"This book on feedback blends grounded science with soulful practicality—nothing wasted, everything intentional. Each chapter feels like a well-placed bassline: subtle, steady, and deeply effective in shifting the rhythm of how we give and receive feedback. It doesn't shout; it hums with wisdom, offering clear, actionable tools that resonate long after the last page."

Chad Thompson, *PhD, Co-Founder and Principal at Mix Talent*

"This book has limitless practical applications and is a universal must read for both personal and professional development. Reading it provided me with an invaluable reframe of how I think about, give, and receive feedback, and the tools and tactics I gained have better equipped me to achieve my own goals as well as empower others to achieve theirs."

Ainsley Daigle, *VP at a music investment/operating firm*

"The science of feedback is complex with multiple dimensions and varieties. Dr. Riordan does a marvelous job breaking it down for us by asking "what is it and how can it impact our lives." If you give, receive, or use feedback (and you likely do ALL 3!), this book is for you. It's also very accessible – a fun read based on the very real science written by a practitioner/scholar who truly believes in the value of feedback and understands the science behind it."

Paul Levy, *PhD, Professor of I/O Psychology, The University of Akron, USA*

"A vital resource for leaders, *Feedback Fundamentals* provides the science-backed blueprint to turn difficult conversations into opportunities for profound growth. It's an essential guide to building more effective, human-centered teams."

Shonna Waters, *PhD*

"*Feedback Fundamentals* by Dr. Brodie Riordan is a rare blend of solid research and real-world practicality. It breaks down the science of feedback into clear, actionable tools that leaders can use right away. I recommend it often to my MBA students – it's a must-read for anyone serious about developing others, and a useful reference guide for anyone navigating real feedback conversations."

Angela Passarelli, *PhD, Associate Professor of Practice, Duke University Fuqua School of Business, USA*

"As an executive coach and talent management leader, I've seen a few characteristics that distinguish top talent from the rest, and one of the most important is a person's ability to leverage feedback to grow themselves and others. The second edition of *Feedback Fundamentals* is the perfect resource for anyone looking to raise their game in work and life. Dr. Brodie Riordan does a masterful job of translating the latest research on feedback into easily understood concepts that can be put into action right away. Feedback Fundamentals (2nd edition) is a must read for any people leader, or anyone interested in growth and development."

Gina Thoebes, *PhD, VP, Organizational Performance Arizona Cardinals Football Club*

"This book is for anyone who has begrudgingly 'given someone the feedback,' felt their heart rate spike when told 'I'd like to share some feedback,' or said, 'thanks for the feedback' while feeling dejected and confused about what to do next. *Feedback Fundamentals* offers actionable strategies for work and life so you can give, ask for, and use feedback with confidence."

Aaron Kraus, *PhD*

Feedback Fundamentals

Now in its second edition, this engaging book takes a deep dive into feedback fundamentals, providing a clear and evidence-based approach to show what makes effective feedback exchanges, and how people can learn and grow from negative feedback, as well as utilize technology to deliver impactful feedback. *Feedback Fundamentals: Give It, Ask for It, Use It* balances research, testimonials, and practical tools to provide readers with a thorough understanding of feedback exchanges.

Critical findings from decades of research in psychology, business, and other disciplines are distilled into tools and strategies that readers can easily adopt in their own lives, regardless of who they are or what they do. Equipped with practical activities, reflective questions, and case studies, this book has a wealth of examples from a variety of people and situations, both within and outside traditional work contexts. This new edition draws together findings from the education context, the COVID-19 pandemic, and the rise of technology to provide easy-to-implement strategies for having thoughtful and constructive conversations about feedback.

Feedback Fundamentals: Give It, Ask for It, Use It is an excellent resource for professionals, leaders, and anyone from any industry or stage in life looking to give better feedback, proactively ask for feedback, gracefully receive feedback, and put that feedback to use.

Brodie Gregory Riordan, PhD, is an industrial/organizational psychologist focused on helping people unlock their potential through coaching, feedback, goal setting, and other best practices from psychological science. She is an executive coach, consultant, and advisor with Ocular, Inc. and BTS, and a part-time faculty member at Georgetown University in Washington, DC, USA.

Feedback Fundamentals

Give It, Ask for It, Use It

Second Edition

BRODIE GREGORY RIORDAN

Routledge
Taylor & Francis Group

NEW YORK AND LONDON

Designed cover image: Getty © Eoneren

Second edition published 2026
by Routledge
605 Third Avenue, New York, NY 10158

and by Routledge
4 Park Square, Milton Park, Abingdon, Oxon, OX14 4RN

Routledge is an imprint of the Taylor & Francis Group, an informa business

© 2026 Taylor & Francis

The right of Brodie Gregory Riordan, to be identified as author of this work has been asserted in accordance with sections 77 and 78 of the Copyright, Designs and Patents Act 1988.

First edition published by Routledge 2021

ISBN: 978-1-032-78163-1 (hbk)
ISBN: 978-1-032-77417-6 (pbk)
ISBN: 978-1-003-48651-0 (ebk)

DOI: 10.4324/9781003486510

Typeset in Sabon and Avenir
by Apex CoVantage, LLC

Contents

Acknowledgments

My mission in writing the first edition of *Feedback Fundamentals* was to share what we know from high-quality, empirical research with readers in a way that is relatable and useful and makes feedback feel less daunting. Research has illuminated so many important nuances, tools, and techniques that make feedback easier to give, ask for, and use. And yet, most of that research rarely gets into the hands and minds of the general public.

Having the opportunity to write a second edition of this book was a gift. In the years since publishing the first edition, I have spent hundreds of hours delivering workshops and having conversations with people about feedback. I have learned so much from these conversations and continued to both refine and expand my own understanding of what makes feedback feel hard and also what makes it much easier to handle.

If you read the first edition, you'll notice some changes. I dropped the chapter on technology and integrated that content throughout the chapters. I pulled in new research from the last few years. I added new visuals and examples. I overhauled Chapters 1 and 2 to make them clearer and more digestible. And, I made sure to preserve the content and concepts that readers found most helpful.

Many people played a role in bringing this book to life. My PhD advisor and frequent collaborator, Paul Levy, initially sent me on this feedback journey. As an editor, Andrew Sylvester helped me with the clarity and conciseness of my writing and was also a critical thought partner on changes to this edition. Nicole Baker has consistently been a terrific partner, helping me with research and other parts of this project. Ali O'Malley has been a steadfast collaborator and sounding board for over 20 years.

Big thanks to the team at Taylor & Francis/Routledge, including Zoe Thomson-Kemp, Shreya Sengupta, Maddie Gray, and Hannah Rich, as well as the team that originally said "yes" to the first edition of this book and helped bring it to life: Christina Chronister, Veronica Morgan, Molly Selby, and Danielle Dyal.

Several generous individuals contributed to this book. Thank you, Adam, Alex, Christopher, David, Finch, Frances, Goodloe, Justice, Nia, and Parker, for participating in interviews and sharing your experiences in this book. Thank you, Gina, Matt, Mel, and Nicole, for providing helpful user tips. And huge thank you to Kristen Van Hise for once again working with me to bring ideas to life through your art.

I am grateful to have family who support, challenge, inspire, and encourage me, particularly my partner, Tim Riordan, who epitomizes patience and support, no matter what I might get myself into.

Feedback Fundamentals   1

In this chapter, we will

- Define what feedback is and is not.
- See that feedback is always in relation to a goal, expectation, or standard.
- Explore the core elements of feedback using a four-part model.

Feedback. It's a loaded word for many people. The mere thought of giving or receiving feedback can elicit an immediate emotional reaction. Often, the first thing that comes to mind when people think about feedback is some formal process, like an annual performance review or an employee feedback survey. But feedback is all around us, all the time. We get feedback from others, from our environment, from technology, and even from ourselves. Giving and receiving feedback are dynamic experiences that shape and are shaped by our relationships and the context of the conversation.

My Mission With This Book

The purpose of this book is to illuminate the value of feedback, the many forms that feedback can take, and just how often we are immersed in feedback in our day-to-day lives. My hope is that by the time you finish this book, you have a new understanding of what exactly feedback is and an appreciation for feedback

DOI: 10.4324/9781003486510-1

as a tool for managing and improving every aspect of your life. I hope that you will find the experience of giving, receiving, asking for, and using feedback to be a little more approachable and less daunting as a result of what you learn in this book and the tools and techniques you'll pick up. This book is intended for anyone who encounters feedback in work or life. Which is pretty much *everyone*. It draws on decades of research findings about what makes feedback work and what gets in the way. My goal is to present these findings in a way that will enable you to apply them in your life and work right away. Over 20 years ago, in the early months of my PhD program, I met with my PhD advisor to talk about the focus for my thesis and ongoing research. When he told me his research focused largely on feedback, I thought to myself, "OMG that is so boring. How can you focus on something as dull and specific as *feedback?*" It wasn't too long before I had a complete change of heart and became his feedback-studying protégé. My initial perception of feedback as a dry, dull, dreadful transaction gradually evolved into seeing it as a rich, complex, and important human interaction. Over the years, I have come to appreciate just how prevalent feedback is and what a difference it can make in people's lives. I have also come to understand how little most of us know about feedback best practices, despite the treasure trove of research from psychology, business, education, and other disciplines. We often talk about feedback in the context of work, but feedback impacts relationships and interactions in all parts of our lives.

The first two chapters of this book cover feedback fundamentals: the basic elements common to all feedback and factors that can get in the way of effective feedback exchanges. The latter chapters explore best practices that you can use right away to effectively give, ask for, receive, and use feedback. In this first chapter, we will spend some time defining feedback. You'll be introduced to the concept of feedback sign, explore the interconnectedness of goals and feedback, and learn the four elements of all feedback exchanges. At the end of every chapter, including this one, you'll find features like "Try It" challenges and pro tips to enhance your experience of using what you learn from this book. You'll also find worksheets and tools in the appendix that you can use to personalize and apply the concepts from this book to your own work and life.

What Feedback Is and What It Isn't

Feedback is simply data about our behaviors. It is inherently backward looking, focusing on things we have done or are doing. Feedback is often provided in an attempt to influence our future behaviors. It provides a way for us to look in the mirror and have a better understanding of what we are doing well and should keep doing, and what is not going well, and we might want to change. Feedback allows us to learn about the impact of our behavior on people and situations, as well as how others perceive us and our behavior. The best feedback is not a judgment, inference, or subjective opinion. It does not focus on the giver's pet peeves or preferences, but rather on objective, observable behaviors that have relevance to or impact on some important goal or expectation. The intent of effective feedback is not to make those receiving it feel small, nor to allow the giver to feel powerful. Feedback is also not advice, though it is often presented that way when people are uncomfortable giving feedback. It feels easier and less intimidating to tell someone what they *should* do next time, rather than telling them about the impact of their past behavior.

Box 1.1

Feedback is simply data about our behaviors. It is inherently backward looking, focusing on things we have done or are doing, with the intention of influencing future behavior.

For example, a leader might receive feedback that they "need to develop their executive presence." That statement might strike you as totally appropriate, and perhaps something you have heard before. But this is not feedback at all—it is advice about what this leader *should* be doing now or in the future. In order to reach this conclusion, the feedback provider likely made some observations, which would actually contribute to *real* feedback—such as, "When this leader gave a presentation yesterday, they looked at the floor the entire time and read very quickly from a script." You can see where that observation might lead someone to the conclusion that this leader "needs to develop their executive presence." The difference is that the observation of the leader's behavior, when provided as feedback, provides specific, evidence-based, behavioral data about what the leader is or is not doing. It's much easier to take action on looking at the floor, reading from a script, and reading quickly, than it is to "develop your presence." Telling a leader that they should develop their presence is flawed not only because it is actually advice (rather than feedback) but also because it is extremely vague. It tells the leader nothing about what they are doing or not doing and why it matters. Research has shown that for adults, activity declines in areas of the brain that are involved in critical thinking and decision making when someone gives them advice (Engelmann et al., 2009). In other words, when we are on the receiving end of advice, we stop actively thinking and engaging and we don't feel a sense of ownership for the ideas that result from it.

Feedback Is Everywhere

As I noted earlier, I have found over the years through my research, consulting work, and teaching that people tend to equate "feedback" with formal and uncomfortable events, like performance reviews. We often fail to recognize feedback as feedback unless it is difficult or uncomfortable to hear. The reality is that we are immersed in feedback of all shapes and sizes, all day, every day. As a demonstration, I decided to record the number of times I had a "feedback event" on a typical day. I found that at the end of the day, I had given, asked for, received, or used feedback 25 times (and I probably missed a few!). As you read my list of feedback experiences below, what do you notice?

1. Data from my Oura ring told me I got 7.5 total hours of sleep, plus how much of that was spent in light, deep, or REM sleep (*received, from technology*).
2. On my morning run, my stiff and aching hamstrings told me I've been sitting too much lately (*received, self-generated*).
3. I asked my partner if my outfit looked okay. He said that the patterns of the shirt and blazer I had on did not match. I agreed and then changed blazers (*asked for, received, and used; from another person*).

4. The chill I felt when I left for work told me I needed a heavier coat and that I should remember to check the weather before I leave the house (*received, from my environment*).
5. The countdown on the "walk" sign told me I needed to hurry up if I wanted to cross the street before the light changed (*received, from my environment*).
6. I told the barista at my local coffee shop that they filled my coffee so high to the top that there was no room for me to add milk (*gave, to another person*).

Once my workday started, the feedback was more likely to involve other people, and technology played a significant role throughout:

7. The 75 new emails in my inbox told me a lot had unfolded since I shut down my laptop yesterday evening (*received, from technology*).
8. On a team call, three colleagues shared helpful input on a document we were writing together, which informed my next round of revisions later that day (*received and used, from other people*).
9. I asked a colleague for his candid reactions to a website my team was developing, and he shared a variety of positive and negative feedback we could use to make the website more tailored to the needs and preferences of our end-users (*asked for and received, from another person*).
10. I asked a few colleagues to weigh in on a budget proposal and share their feedback on where and how certain allocations are being made (*asked for, from other people*).
11. A colleague told me that a recent survey I sent out lacked a "Not Applicable" option, which made it hard to respond to some items (*received, from another person*).
12. An instant message from a colleague told me that I was nine minutes late to a conference call (*received, from another person via technology*).
13. My Apple Watch told me I had been sitting for nearly two hours without getting up (*received, from technology*).
14. A colleague reminded me that the paper handouts I was planning to take to a conference violated the conference's paperless initiative (*received, from another person*).

15. A designer shared an updated version of a visual document, and I provided her with a few changes to make in the next round (*gave, to another person*).
16. I used an online feedback tool to formally recognize four teammates for work they did launching a program that impacted 16,000 colleagues (*gave, to other people*).
17. A team member asked for feedback on a document for our leadership team; I told her what was strong and high impact about the document, shared negative feedback on two sections that were unclear, and thanked her for taking the lead on it (*gave, in response to being asked, to another person*).

And the feedback continued into the evening:

18. My yoga teacher asked for feedback on a new sequence of poses and her new playlist; I told her the sequence left my quads and triceps burning and that the tone and tempo of the playlist complemented the sequence (*gave, in response to being asked, to another person*).
19. A light came on the dashboard of my car telling me that I was following too close to the car in front of me, so I slowed down and put more distance between us (*received, from technology, and used*).
20. The director of a non-profit whose board I'm on emailed to apologize for taking a while to send me a document. I told her that her timing was fine, and I wouldn't be able to review it until the weekend anyway (*gave, to another person*).
21. I commented on my niece's Instagram post with positive feedback about the picture she posted (*gave, to another person*).
22. I read online reviews of the two restaurants I was considering for dinner and made a choice based on other users' reviews and photos (*used, via technology, technically from other people but all strangers*).
23. I sent a thank you note to a friend giving them positive feedback on an event they had recently hosted. I noticed I started with platitudes and pushed myself to be specific in my feedback (*gave, to another person*).
24. A Duo Lingo notification reminded me that I had not completed a Spanish lesson for the day and risked breaking my 800+ day streak (*received, from technology*).

25. My partner told me that when I ask him a question and then proceed to answer it myself, he isn't sure what I am looking for from him (*received, from another person*).

As you read that list, how many of those examples felt scary, threatening, or judgmental? How many of these examples seemed so mundane and routine that you likely would have overlooked them as feedback at all? To me, they look, feel, and sound like *data*. I experienced each of these feedback moments as helpful and constructive. Nothing triggered a strong emotional reaction, insulted me or hurt my feelings, or resulted in inconvenience or major changes in direction for whatever I was working on. Contrast this with the results from an informal survey that I conducted: I asked over 1,000 people about their immediate reaction when they hear the words "feedback" or "let me give you some feedback." Across cultures, industries, ages, genders, and experiences, I consistently found that about 70% react in a decidedly negative way. He's a sample of the responses I received:

- "No specific words come to mind, but I get this feeling in my body—like I raise and tighten my shoulders, I feel like I'm bristling."
- "My first instinct is, 'I wonder what I did wrong!'"
- "Yikes! Duck and wait for criticism."
- "Brace yourself!"
- "Ugh!"
- "Sweaty palms, racing heart, fake smile, 'sure, I'd love to hear it.'"
- "I steel myself to hear something negative."
- "I overthink it and my anxiety hits the roof even though I know feedback is a gift."

Some people described their reaction as a Pavlovian[1] response. Simply hearing the word "feedback" evokes an instant physical and emotional reaction in them. "Feedback" is a powerful word and loaded with baggage from unpleasant past experiences if it can elicit that kind of immediate response. It doesn't have to be this way. People are not born dreading feedback; their attitudes develop over time based on their experiences, something we'll explore more later in this chapter. Feedback is a highly useful source of information. It helps us navigate the world around us, our relationships, and our social interactions. It allows us to be more self-aware, gauge progress toward goals, learn what we are doing well and should keep doing, and identify things we might want to do differently. Feedback provides the information necessary to perform at a higher level, achieve goals, grow, and have deeper self-understanding. But for people who actively dislike feedback and dread receiving it, that value is lost.

Goals, Expectations, and Standards: Feedback Is Always in Relation to *Something*

One often overlooked fact is that feedback is always in relation to *something*. Feedback arises because we, someone else, or technology detect a gap between some standard or expectation and reality. For example, earlier today I ate a cookie. When I took the first bite I said (literally, out loud), "Wow, that is a really good cookie." If I had actually said that to the baker, it would be an example of positive feedback. I had an implicit expectation of what the cookie would taste like, based on how it looked and where I purchased it, but the actual flavor and consistency of the cookie exceeded my expectations. Take a moment and think about a piece of feedback you recently gave someone or received; what was the underlying goal, standard, or expectation that the feedback was in relation to? For example, if your manager gives you feedback on opportunities to improve your presentation skills, your boss is comparing your *actual* presentation skills to some standard or expectation they have for what "good presentation skills" entail. Those expectations are not always clearly communicated or shared, which is why feedback can sometimes catch us by surprise or sound like an opinion.

Human behavior is consistently driven and motivated by goals. When I say goals, I mean both the formal, structured goals you set at work and all of the tiny goals you might not even be aware of that drive your behavior every single day. Some of those goals are explicit—those that we deliberately set, actively track, and may even share with others, such as saving a certain amount of money by the end of the year, meditating for 30 consecutive days, or finally being able to do 25 push-ups without stopping. But many of our goals are implicit. Perhaps the reason you brush your teeth at night is to have good dental health, to avoid a costly trip to the dentist, or to have fresher breath. Whatever your goal, you probably don't actively think about it every morning and night, yet it drives you to brush your teeth. When we are motivated to do something, some goal is driving that behavior. Goals and feedback are deeply intertwined. Feedback is a critical mechanism for assessing progress toward achieving goals. Feedback—whether it comes from other people, our environment (e.g., a scale, a car speedometer), our bodies (e.g., pain, hunger, temperature), or our own inner monologue—tells us where we stand in relation to goals, expectations, and standards.

Research on Feedback Intervention Theory (FIT; Kluger & Denisi, 1996) identified important conditions that determine whether or not feedback has a positive impact on people's behavior and performance. This theory suggests that people regulate their behavior and gain self-awareness by comparing feedback about their current behavior to a set of standards or expectations. These expectations or standards can be self-generated or come from someone else, such as a boss, partner, or parent. When we detect a discrepancy between our current behavior and the standard or expectation, we are motivated to change our behavior (or, in some cases, change the goal or standard—more on that in Chapter 5) to close the gap. Receiving feedback on that specific behavior directs our attention toward the behavior, which increases the likelihood we'll notice what we need to change (self-awareness) and then make the change in our future behavior. Feedback Intervention Theory has roots in another classic theory, Control Theory, which provides one of my favorite metaphors for thinking about feedback: a thermostat.

Like a Thermostat

Imagine a thermostat: You set a desired temperature, and the system responds by sensing the current room temperature and adjusting accordingly to close the gap between the current temperature and the desired temperature. This is an example of a basic control loop, which is also how feedback operates in conjunction with standards, goals, and expectations. Feedback tells us the distance between our current state and that target state we are trying to achieve. For example, let's consider Pat, who is trying to maintain a body weight of 150 pounds. When Pat steps on the scale, they receive feedback about where they stand with respect to that goal: the distance between their current state (current weight) and their desired state (150 pounds). The *direction* of that gap will vary based on Pat's starting weight relative to the goal. If Pat's goal is to be at or below 150 pounds, and the scale reads 160, then the scale is giving Pat *negative* feedback that they have a 10-pound gap between their current and desired state. On the other hand, if the scale reads 148 pounds, Pat gets *positive* feedback; their current state (148 pounds) is at or below their goal weight of 150 pounds. Notice that in this example *negative feedback* simply means that there is a gap between Pat's current state and their goal, whereas *positive feedback* results when Pat has hit or come in below their goal weight of 150 pounds. Positive and negative here refer to the *sign* of the feedback, something we'll discuss in more detail later in this chapter. On the other hand, if Pat's goal was to gain weight and get *above* 150 pounds, then the signs of the feedback would be reversed, such that weighing in at 148 pounds would now be considered *negative feedback* (because Pat had not reached their goal of a minimum of 150 pounds) and a reading on the scale of 152 would be *positive feedback* because Pat has met or exceeded their goal of weighing at least 150 pounds. As you can see, the sign of feedback is relative to both the standard and the starting point.

Control theory is a theory of motivation—it is predicated on the idea that we are motivated to achieve goals, and our ability to assess the distance between our current state and desired goal state fuels us to act (Carver & Scheier, 1998; see Figure 1.1 for a visual example). Control theory provides a structured framework for thinking about feedback in any context. Any goal, project, or aspiration that you have can be mapped to control theory. Think about a goal you have right now—can you map it to a basic control loop? What is your current state? What is your goal? When you compare those two, what feedback are you generating or receiving about the distance between your current and desired state, and how you can close that gap? Use the worksheet in Appendix A to apply control theory to your own example.

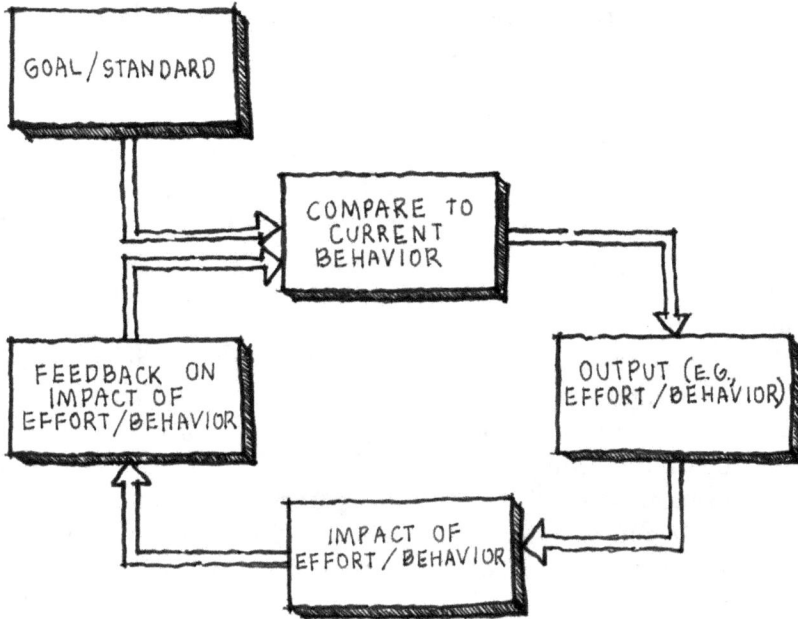

Figure 1.1 Feedback and goals operate like a control loop—just like the thermostat in your house.

Here's another example of a control loop, this time applied to a work context. Whitney is a senior manager in the finance group at her organization (current state). She wants to be promoted into a director role in the group (her goal/desired state). Whitney uses a few sources of feedback to help her know where she stands in her pursuit of this goal:

- Self-generated feedback: There is an open director position in her group. Whitney compares her education, skills, and prior experiences to the qualifications listed in the job description. This generates positive feedback, because she sees that she meets all of those qualifications.
- Feedback from others: Whitney's manager told her in a performance review that she has fully mastered her current role and should think about what she wants to do next. Whitney's HR business partner also thinks Whitney meets the qualifications for the director role and encourages her to apply. Comments from Whitney's manager and HR partner constitute positive

feedback because they indicate that she is meeting the standards necessary for the desired promotion.

Based on these data points, Whitney believes that she is very close to closing the gap between her current state and her goal of moving into the director role. She feels energized and excited by the momentum and takes actions that are within her control to close the gap (updating her resume, letting her manager know she is interested in the role, reaching out to the hiring manager, officially applying for the job).

Because feedback helps us gauge where we stand in pursuit of our goals and things that are important to us (see Figure 1.2), it serves an important motivating (or demotivating) function. In fact, the combination of goals and feedback together has a more powerful motivating effect than either of the two alone (Locke & Latham, 2019). Generally, as people get closer to achieving their goal, they experience a spike in motivation, encouraging them through the final push. Making progress more rapidly than anticipated may even inspire us to revise our goals to be more challenging (Locke & Latham, 2002). But when feedback indicates that we are not making progress and closing the gap to reach our goal, we are more likely to feel deflated and demotivated, which might lead us to engage in behaviors that further slow our progress. In Chapter 5, we'll further explore the relationship between goals and feedback, goal setting, and the impact of goals on our motivation and behavior, and we'll explore how negative feedback is actually beneficial to this process by helping to redirect and refocus our efforts

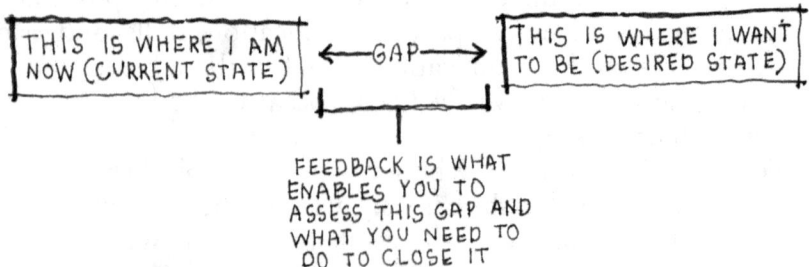

Figure 1.2 Feedback tells you about the gap between where you are now and where you want to be.

Feedback enables increased self-awareness and tells us what we need to do to elevate our performance or be better at just about anything. Without feedback, our efforts occur in a vacuum. We lack visibility into how close or far we are from attaining our goals, and therefore if our level of effort is appropriate, too little, or too great. Positive feedback lets us know when we are closing in on or have achieved our goal; it can be a tremendous source of positive emotion. Negative feedback, though it often gets a bad rap, allows us to assess what we need to do to get closer to our goals, have higher performance, learn, and grow. Now that we have established what feedback is and is not, and that it's always in relation to something (a goal, standard, or expectation), we'll shift our attention to the core elements of feedback, summarized in a four-part model that can be applied to all feedback exchanges.

Four Elements of Any Feedback Exchange

Although both giving and receiving feedback can feel daunting, when we break it down into its core elements, even the most challenging feedback discussion can feel a little less intimidating. Recognizing the building blocks of feedback and where things could derail (such as what you say, how you say it, when and where you say it, what medium you use to communicate it, etc.) diminishes some of the risk and uncertainty. Every feedback exchange—no matter who is involved, how minor or serious the topic, or whether the feedback is positive or negative—consists of four elements: The feedback provider or "source," the actual message, the context in which it is provided, and the perceptions and attitudes of the recipient (Gregory & Levy, 2015[2]). This sounds simple enough, but a deeper look at each of these four elements reveals important nuances that impact the effectiveness of the feedback exchange. The ultimate goals of feedback are to help people become more self-aware, understand how they are currently doing with respect to goals or expectations, and do more of something, less of something, or something altogether different in the future. Achieving these goals depends on whether or not the recipient will accept the feedback in the first place. All four elements of the model (see Figure 1.3) impact the likelihood that someone will accept and use feedback.

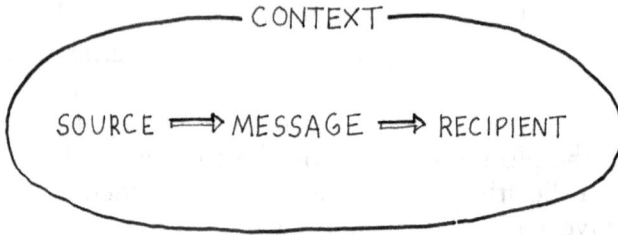

Figure 1.3 All feedback exchanges consist of four elements.
(Gregory & Levy, 2015). Reprinted with permission from APA.

The Feedback Source

All feedback comes from someone or something. Much of the feedback we process throughout the day is self-generated (e.g., your inner monologue) or comes from our environment. But often the feedback that stands out most, and can feel either most fulfilling or emotionally challenging, is feedback from other people. But not all feedback providers are created equal. Attributes of feedback providers, as well as our history and relationships with them, influence our perceptions of their feedback. All feedback exchanges between two people occur in the context of everything that has happened in their relationship up to that moment, and each exchange will impact their relationship going forward.

Research has consistently shown that feedback is most likely to be accepted and put to use when the person providing it is perceived to be credible—that they are trustworthy and have some expertise on the topic at hand (Baker et al., 2025; Ilgen et al., 1979; Kraus, 2024; Vancouver & Morrison, 1995). In other words, the recipient trusts the provider and thinks they know what they are talking about. For example, I interviewed David, a Grammy Award-winning musician and producer, who remarked that critical feedback from a credible source with great experience and a great ear goes a really long way, whereas feedback from someone who lacks experience or whose perspective he doesn't trust lands very differently with him. David explains,

> A really good producer is able to give useful feedback, including hard truths. It's easy to be a "yes man" and just

tell people they are brilliant; it's hard to say "this isn't your best work—you can do better. Specifically on XYZ." On the other hand, I have a musician friend who is a great musician, but we have very different perspectives. When we don't agree on things, I know I'm on the right track. He always gives me negative feedback on my best work. It helps to know where people are coming from.

Feedback is more likely to be seen as accurate when provided by a credible source (Albright & Levy, 1995), and when feedback is seen as accurate, it's more likely to be accepted and used. People are also more motivated to use feedback when they believe that the provider is competent in whatever domain is being discussed (Steelman et al., 2004). One study found that the perceived credibility of the feedback provider mattered more than the delivery format (e.g., email vs. video call) for how the feedback was received (Baker et al., 2025). In other words, if someone gives you feedback and you believe that they have some credibility and expertise related to the topic of the feedback, you will be more likely to believe that they know what they are talking about, that their feedback is "true" or accurate, and therefore you'll be more likely to accept and do something with that feedback. In David's example, a producer or collaborator builds credibility and trust when they have demonstrated a track record of helpful feedback and good judgment.

Feedback does not occur in a vacuum. It's not simply a one-time transaction, although some people treat it as such. Any exchange of feedback between two people is a human interaction steeped in the emotions, history, and expectations we have of one another. Not only does the existing relationship between the feedback provider and feedback recipient affect the dynamics and impact of a feedback discussion, that feedback discussion also contributes to and shapes the future of the relationship. Recipients are more likely to see feedback as fair and feel more motivated to use it when it comes from a source with whom they have a positive relationship (Pat El et al., 2012; Sparr & Sonnentag, 2008). Who provides feedback and the way they share it can either build trust and enhance the relationship over time, or quickly erode a relationship (Katz et al., 2023; London et al., 2023).

The Message

What the feedback source says and how they frame it impacts what we hear, how we react to it, and what we choose to do with it. This second element of the four-part feedback model is the message, or the actual content of what is shared in the feedback exchange. The devil is in the details when it comes to the content of the message. Characteristics like the focus of the feedback (person vs. behavior) and the level of specificity, among others, influence how the message comes across to the recipient. Often a feedback provider has good intentions and useful data they want to share, but gets tripped up in their word choice, clarity, and how little or much they say. For now, we'll focus on some of the most essential distinctions of the feedback message.

Feedback Sign

All feedback is either positive or negative, which we refer to as the *sign* of the feedback. You'll recall from earlier in this chapter that the reason feedback is always either positive or negative is because it tells you how you are doing relative to some standard, goal, or expectation. Positive feedback simply means that the feedback is telling you something favorable—that you have met or exceeded the standard, achieved your goal, or are performing according to or above expectations. Positive feedback tells someone their efforts are paying off and may indicate that no additional work is needed to achieve a goal; it is likely to elicit positive emotions (Anseel & Lievens, 2006). Negative feedback highlights a deficit or gap between someone's current state or current level of performance and the goal or standard that their performance is being compared to. Negative feedback is often misconstrued as "feedback delivered poorly" and, therefore, referred to instead by names like "constructive feedback" or "constructive criticism." Although negative feedback can elicit strong emotions or feelings of being threatened (particularly when it is delivered poorly or unskillfully), it actually has a great deal of utility (Abi-Esber et al., 2022; Medvedeff et al., 2008). Negative feedback tells us what we need to do to close the gap between where we are and where we want to be; it can provide a roadmap of what you need to do more of, less of, or differently to grow or have stronger performance. You'll notice in this book I consistently use the terms positive and negative, as opposed to "praise" or "constructive criticism." Positive and negative feedback are technical terms that describe the behavior relative to the goal or expectation. I use these terms throughout the book because they are clear and direct, and also to avoid suggesting that positive feedback is good and negative feedback is bad.

When faced with providing negative feedback, many people stall, avoid giving it, or provide it in a way that is so diluted or sandwiched between positive feedback that the recipient is left completely unclear on what the real issue is, why it matters, and what they should do about it. This discomfort providing negative feedback results in a loss for everyone involved. The person providing the feedback misses an opportunity to share their valuable perspective, help another person grow and improve, and potentially highlight a blind spot for that person. The person who would be the target of the feedback misses out on valuable information that would help them better understand their current level of performance, and how close or far their current state is from their goals. Without negative feedback, we are blind to what we need to do better or how we can close in on our goals. In later chapters about giving and asking for feedback, we'll explore ways to make providing and receiving negative feedback feel less daunting and more productive.

The Focus of the Feedback

Feedback can focus on the person as a person or it can focus on their observable behavior or some task they have performed. Person-focused feedback refers to who the receiver is as a person—their capabilities, personality, or character—whereas behavior-focused feedback refers to their observable actions or behaviors. Person-focused feedback may sound like "You are disorganized and unreliable"—big labels to put on the person. But what was the behavior that led the provider to that conclusion? Perhaps simply, "You did not send me the completed document by 5 pm, as we had agreed." You can see where the feedback provider might generalize this behavior to a conclusion that someone is unreliable and disorganized, but sharing this conclusion as person-focused feedback is unhelpful and hard for the receiver to translate into action. This negative person-focused feedback feels like a judgment or character attack. People are more likely to get defensive and reject negative feedback that focuses on them as a person, as opposed to their behavior. Not only is it less likely to be accepted, it's also *harder* to use!

Holding up the mirror and sharing the data that the person did not send the completed document by 5 pm focuses on observable behavior, which is much easier to change or act on next time the situation arises. This feedback might sound different than what you are accustomed to. It might sound a little dry and basic, but that's actually a good thing. Behavior-focused feedback is much less likely to elicit a strong emotional reaction, compared with labels, such as "disorganized" and "unreliable." Feedback that focuses on actions or behaviors is more likely to be accepted and also more conducive to future behavior change. It is much easier to change your behavior (send the completed document on time or agree to a more realistic deadline) than to change who you are as a person (unreliable and disorganized).

The benefits of behavior-focused feedback don't just pertain to negative feedback. Research by Carol Dweck of Stanford University and her collaborators has shown that providing positive feedback on someone's abilities (person-focused) can make that person less resilient to future challenges because they attribute their success to their abilities, rather than their hard work or effort (Dweck, 2006). Person-focused positive feedback, though well-intended, does not help people learn what it was they did well to contribute to positive outcomes. You have probably been on the receiving end of person-focused positive feedback throughout your entire life. It's common to hear parents tell their children how smart they are or what a good basketball player they are, or for bosses to tell their top performers that they are "rockstars," "brilliant," or "amazing." Though these platitudes may sound nice, they tell the recipient little to nothing about their behavior or how that behavior contributed to their success. This empty-calorie feedback wastes the opportunity to help the receiver understand *what* exactly they did that was positive, and *why* it mattered. Next time you are tempted to tell a colleague or friend that they are "awesome" or "amazing," push yourself to let them know what exactly they did that led you to that conclusion.

This touches on another important element of the message: specificity. In general, the more specific feedback is, the easier it is to understand and use. Humans often think in generalities, or at a high level of abstraction, and need to push ourselves to identify specific, observable behaviors if we want to give high-quality, useful feedback. Feedback can also be framed in terms of a work in progress or an evaluation of something that is complete. Feedback focused on how you're doing on something you're currently working on is known as *process feedback* and feedback that provides an overall evaluation of how you did once something is complete is referred to as *outcome feedback*. Process feedback is more conducive to behavior change and immediate course correction, whereas outcome feedback feels like a final evaluation. As we'll see in Chapter 2, these two types of feedback (they are, in fact, referred to as "feedback type") have a significant impact on how we react to feedback—particularly when we cross these types with feedback sign (positive vs. negative).

Context

Where, when, and how feedback is provided—the context— influences how feedback is perceived and received. In general, feedback should be provided as soon as possible after an event occurs, while the event is still fresh in the minds of the giver and the recipient (Hays et al., 2013; van der Kleij et al., 2012). If the purpose of feedback is to help people adjust their behavior to be more effective, timely feedback enables prompt behavior change and is more likely to result in improved performance. One exception to the "as soon as possible" rule is to wait until feedback can be provided in a private setting (Ashford & Northcraft, 1992; Delavallade, 2021). Receiving feedback in public can be uncomfortable and activate self-consciousness in the recipient—it can take their attention away from improving their behavior and instead focuses their attention inward to their own discomfort and insecurities, something we'll see more about in Chapter 3.

Feedback providers have choice about when and where to provide feedback and also must consider what medium will be most effective given the situation. We have a multitude of choices in how and when to provide feedback. In many modern workplaces, feedback providers can choose from video conferencing (such as Zoom or Microsoft Teams), phone calls, written feedback (such as comments on a document or sending an email), and immediate methods like texting, Slack, or instant message. Every medium has pros and cons, and the key to choosing an effective delivery method is aligning the goals and sensitivity of the topic with the advantages of the delivery method. For example, I interviewed Frances, a family law attorney in Paris, who occasionally chooses to text her clients if she needs to give them immediate feedback to change their behavior when a situation is escalating. Given her goal of alerting the client about their behavior immediately, texting is an appropriate choice. A more extensive face-to-face or phone discussion of the client's behavior typically follows, but texting enables immediate feedback and course correction. Texting feedback can also be appropriate for time-sensitive but low-stakes feedback, such as alerting a colleague who is on their way to an important client meeting that they have spinach in their teeth or that they routinely call the client Sara when, in fact, her name is Tara.

The context in which feedback is provided also includes the overall environment. Intangibles, such as a culture of psychological safety and learning, significantly impact the success of a feedback exchange. Researcher Amy Edmondson (1999; also Edmondson & Bransby, 2023) notes that organizations with high levels of psychological safety—where individuals feel comfortable being themselves, taking risks, or making mistakes—better support feedback seeking and learning. When people experience a sense of psychological safety, they are less likely to worry about being judged, embarrassed, or punished for their behavior. As a result, they are more likely to set challenging goals, speak up, ask for help, and take risks (Edmondson & Bransby, 2023; Li & Tan, 2013). The concept of psychological safety is closely aligned with the idea of learning cultures, which promote growth, development, self-awareness, and improved performance by empowering individuals to feel supported in taking risks, making mistakes, and giving, receiving, and asking for feedback. *Learning cultures* promote inquiry and dialogue (Yang et al., 2004) and encourage people to ask for feedback and experiment with behaviors (London, 2003), whereas *performance cultures* focus disproportionately on demonstrating and proving competence.

Additionally, every organization has a *feedback environment* that influences norms and behaviors related to giving, accepting, and using feedback (London & Smither, 2002; Steelman et al., 2004). The feedback environment is part of the intangible culture that is created by and constantly evolving as a result of leader and employee behaviors. An organization's feedback environment is shaped both from the top down (leaders impacting the rest of the organization) and from the bottom up (employees' day-to-day feedback behavior shaping the overall culture). In a favorable feedback environment, colleagues regularly give, ask for, and apply feedback. They see feedback as a way to grow and improve performance and to communicate effectively with their colleagues. On the other hand, employees in organizations with unfavorable feedback environments hesitate to seek out or offer feedback. Asking for or receiving feedback may be perceived as a sign of weakness, self-doubt, or low performance. The feedback environment where someone works can shape (and be shaped by) their personal attitudes toward feedback. Working in an organization with a favorable feedback environment can help individuals strengthen and develop their own *feedback orientation*, a concept we'll discuss in the next section. Since a feedback environment can develop from the bottom up, having critical mass of employees with strong feedback orientations can drive a stronger organizational feedback environment over time.

The Recipient

Humans are complex, multi-faceted, and shaped by years of past experiences, all of which influence how a person responds to feedback. Individual differences and attitudes, like self-efficacy, personality, and learning orientation, all impact how people think about, behave, and respond to feedback. In the early 2000s, researchers conceived of an individual difference, which they named *feedback orientation*, that specifically pertains to people's attitudes and behaviors related to feedback. Every person has a feedback orientation that underlies how they think about, feel about, and are motivated to use feedback (Linderbaum & Levy, 2010; London & Smither, 2002). This orientation is shaped by past experiences with feedback, for better or for worse. Feedback orientation is disproportionately influenced by the teachers, coaches, parents, bosses, and colleagues who give us feedback over the course of our lives, many of whom are just as uncomfortable providing feedback as they are receiving it. In addition to being uncomfortable, chances are they are also unskilled. As you'll see over the next four chapters, the ability to give, receive, ask for, and use feedback is learned. If you want to engage skillfully with feedback, you have to invest time and effort into learning the specific nuances that make feedback effective and then have the courage to give or ask for the feedback. Feedback orientation is a dynamic attitude that can be strengthened and developed over time, particularly when someone works in a favorable feedback environment, and learns or chooses to like, value, use, and proactively seek out feedback (Linderbaum & Levy, 2010). A strong feedback orientation has been linked to higher job performance, greater citizenship behaviors at work, higher job satisfaction, greater role clarity, seeking more feedback, and other positive workplace behaviors (Katz et al., 2023). On the other hand, having a weak feedback orientation can translate to avoiding, disliking, and disregarding others' feedback.

Another individual difference that impacts how people think and feel about feedback is self-efficacy. Self-efficacy pertains to a person's belief that they are capable of achieving their goals or completing whatever task is in front of them (Bandura, 1986), and specifically *feedback self-efficacy* is a sub-dimension of feedback orientation (Linderbaum & Levy, 2010). Someone who has a strong sense of self-efficacy believes that they can achieve important outcomes through their choices and behaviors, and that they have some control over what happens in their work and life. We develop this belief over time by demonstrating to ourselves what we are capable of. Self-efficacy can also pertain to specific domains or situations. For example, a student who has worked hard over the years to develop their programming skills may have high self-efficacy about their ability to program and troubleshoot technology. However, they may have had less success or exposure to creative writing courses and have invested less time in creative writing, and therefore have a lower sense of self-efficacy about their creative writing skills. Those feelings of self-efficacy impact future behaviors, such as how likely that student will be to pursue creative writing courses or projects compared with programming and tech-related opportunities. That sense of self-efficacy will also impact the extent to which that person is resilient to, sees the value in, and uses feedback, particularly negative feedback. When we have higher self-efficacy, that negative feedback feels less threatening, and we are more likely to see it as a tool to help us continue to learn, grow, and improve. Because high self-efficacy equates to a belief that our actions can influence outcomes, we are more likely to believe that we can do something with the negative feedback to strengthen future behavior or performance. Positive feedback also has the potential to build self-efficacy over time by helping us see the impact of our efforts.

Other personal attitudes and attributes affect our feedback behavior, such as whether we are more focused on learning (learning oriented) or demonstrating our competence (performance oriented). Just as organizations can be more oriented toward learning or performance, so too can individuals. Performance orientation is a specific term in psychology meant to describe people who are primarily focused on demonstrating their competence, as opposed to learning and growing while also doing great work. Motivation to perform at a high level is not a bad thing, but a singular focus on proving yourself (or avoiding looking incompetent) and how much you know actually gets in the way of learning, growing, and, ironically, performing at a high level (VandeWalle et al., 2001). People who are learning- and growth-oriented value feedback as a way to become more self-aware, to learn from their actions and behaviors, and to identify opportunities to be more effective in the future. On the other hand, a performance-oriented person who is motivated to demonstrate their competence will typically perceive negative feedback as a threat, rather than as valuable data. For performance-oriented individuals, negative feedback tells them that they haven't done everything just right, which diminishes their sense of competence.

Personality also plays a role in how people hear and respond to feedback. People high in trait anxiety or neuroticism (one of the Big Five personality variables, a common framework for describing personality along five dimensions) are less likely to accept, use, and ask for feedback, whereas people high in the Big Five personality dimension of conscientiousness tend to be more motivated to put feedback to use, resulting in higher performance (Colquitt et al., 2000; Dominick et al., 2004). The remaining dimensions of the Big Five personality framework (openness to experience, agreeableness, and extraversion) have not been as consistently linked to feedback attitudes and behaviors as neuroticism and conscientiousness. Personality attributes change little across our lifetime, whereas attitudes, like feedback orientation, self-efficacy, and learning orientation can be cultivated and developed through time, experience, and intention. Our feedback behavior is influenced by these attributes and attitudes, and feedback can also help to *strengthen* those attitudes. High self-efficacy leads us to value feedback, and receiving and using high-quality feedback can further strengthen our sense of self-efficacy, creating a virtuous cycle. People can make an intentional choice to strengthen their feedback orientation and related attitudes, putting them on a path to being more learning- and growth-oriented and more self-aware. In order to get there, they have to realize they can make that choice and also be willing to embrace the temporary discomfort of accepting and asking for feedback more often.

Applying the Four-Element Model

Think about a recent feedback experience you've had. Can you map that experience to this four-part feedback model? If the feedback exchange didn't go particularly well, where did the breakdown occur? In instances where you received feedback, did the problem stem from the feedback source—who gave you the feedback, your relationship with them, your perceptions of them or their behavior? Was it what they said (message) or when, where, or how they provided it (context)? As the feedback recipient, what role did you play in the success or failure of the feedback exchange? How did your own feedback orientation or attitudes influence your reaction to the feedback?

This four-part model helps us break down and think through any feedback exchange, no matter how difficult or mundane it may be. For example, imagine you are staying in an Airbnb that you booked. You saw a mouse in the kitchen during your stay, and you want to give the owners feedback about it. Let's apply the four-part model. Since you are the one sharing the feedback, you are the *source*. Recall that trust and credibility are some of the most important attributes of the feedback source. You have credibility with the owners because you have a five-star rating on Airbnb and have been a respectful tenant adhering to the guidelines and terms of the rental. You have built trust with the owners through your interactions so far, such as being clear and prompt in your communication and paying on time.

Now you need to decide how to frame your *message*. You want to be specific, evidence-based, and focused on observable behaviors. That might sound like, "This morning when I was making breakfast in the kitchen around 7:30 am a mouse ran across the kitchen, from under the stove to behind the refrigerator." And stop there. This is where many people make mistakes in their feedback. You might feel tempted to make inferences about why, or draw some kind of conclusion, but if you really want to give clear, direct, evidence-based feedback you will stop with that statement. Let the recipient take the feedback and decide how to respond and what to do next. Unless they have proven otherwise, assume they are responsive and responsible adults who can solve their own problems—this is an important part of thinking about the *recipient* in how you frame your message. Once you provide the feedback, the recipient owns what they will do with it. They get to choose how to respond, which could include dismissing your feedback, taking immediate action, asking clarifying questions, or getting into an argument or debate with you.

This is where *context* comes into play. In this example, you provide your feedback using the Airbnb online messaging app. Because you are not talking face to face or on the phone with the owners, it's important that your message is clear and direct. If this was the third time you shared the feedback about seeing the mouse, and the owners have previously been unresponsive or did not take action, now you know more about them (the feedback recipient) and may need to adjust your approach. For instance, you could follow with an expectation, such as, "Owner, this is the third time I have seen a mouse in the kitchen, and you have not addressed the problem. If you don't respond about the mouse problem in the kitchen I will file a complaint with Airbnb." This highlights another aspect of *context*. The internet age has obscured the distinction between private feedback and public reviews. Remember, people are much more likely to hear and accept feedback when it is provided privately. The first time you see the mouse, you want to ensure you share the feedback privately, such as communicating via the Airbnb app messaging system, texting, or talking to them on the phone. If you get to a point where they are unresponsive and you need to escalate your feedback, you can add that you will "mention this in my review of your unit," thereby taking your feedback public and potentially impacting the appeal of their Airbnb rental for future tenants.

This four-part feedback model can be used as a tool to plan and structure any feedback that you need to provide. In Appendix B, you'll find a set of questions that you can use to apply the four-element model to your own feedback exchanges. Feedback feels less intimidating when we parse it out into component parts and use a structure to think through exactly what we want to say, when, where, and how we want to say it. This model also makes the feedback recipient an important part of the equation. When you're on the receiving end of feedback, it is easy to feel like the feedback conversation is "happening to" you. Many people fail to recognize that as the recipient they can elect to take an active role in the conversation and turn it into a dialogue. Consider Christopher, an alumni team member of Back on My Feet,[3] who has learned over time how to participate more in feedback conversations and respond in a way that feels productive. In our interview, Christopher remarked that when receiving feedback in the past, he would simply take the feedback at face value and deal with his inner turmoil about it. Now he notices his own thoughts and feelings and engages with the feedback provider more pro-actively. Says Christopher,

> When receiving feedback, I used to be more reactive. I would push away and bury problems and conflict, not face them. Then those problems would escalate. I still have emotional reactions when I hear feedback, that feeling like I'm being judged. But now I know how to recognize my reaction and pause. I say to myself, "I feel like I'm being judged. Am I being judged? What is this person's perspective?" Then I'll ask them questions to better understand where they are coming from.

Once a feedback provider offers their observations, the recipient can choose how they want to respond. They can see the feedback exchange as a one-way transaction by simply accepting what the other person has said without engaging further or asking questions. Or, like Christopher, they can pause, recognize their reaction, and take ownership for their experience. Remember that most people are both uncomfortable and unskilled at giving feedback. By adopting an ownership mindset for your experience of receiving feedback, you can assume the other person has something useful to tell you even if they are not doing a great job of communicating it to you. By asking curious questions and turning your conversation into a dialogue, you increase the likelihood that you will leave the conversation with valuable new data and insights.

Wrapping Up

In this chapter, we took a look at what feedback is, and what it is not. We explored theories that show how feedback is always in relation to something, such as a goal, standard, or expectation. We demonstrated how all feedback exchanges can be broken down into four elements: the source of the feedback, the actual message, the context in which that message is provided, and the feedback recipient. Without feedback, we would be adrift in a world with little context or direction. Imagine a world where you had no idea how you were doing in school, in your job performance, in your marriage—where you didn't know how others perceived you or the impact you were having on them. What could be possible if you gave all of that (helpful and well-intended!) feedback you've been holding inside for so long: for the coworker who doesn't realize his phone voice sounds like shouting, for your spouse who has not finished that project started long ago, for your friend who continues to make poor dating decisions? And what if they told you all the things they've been holding inside: How you get very quiet in meetings with senior leadership, that you say "you know" a lot when you make presentations, that the haircut you had last summer was the perfect fit for your face shape? When well-intended, useful feedback flows freely, everyone has a clearer understanding of how they are impacting and impacted by the world around them. Feedback given the right way doesn't feel jarring or painful and can truly help people have increased self-awareness and grow and develop. Decades of research on feedback have shown us what makes feedback most effective and easy to receive, but that research rarely makes it from academic journals to everyday life. In Chapter 2, we'll take a closer look at what can get in the way of people giving, asking for, accepting, and using feedback.

Try It

Pick a day and log all of your feedback experiences. Note every time you give, receive, ask for, or use feedback. What do you notice? How many of those experiences are "formal" feedback exchanges versus relatively mundane? What surprises you about your day of feedback?

Pro Tip

If you find yourself giving advice or telling someone what they *should* do, pause and ask yourself, "What is the actual behavior I have seen in this person that leads me to give this advice?" Rather than giving the advice, hold up the mirror to them by sharing the data-based feedback on what you actually observed in their behavior. Jump ahead to Chapter 3 to learn more about best practices for giving feedback.

Notes

1 Pavlov was a behavioral psychologist who found that, after consistently pairing their dinner with the ringing of a bell, dogs would eventually begin to salivate at the sound of the bell, even when no food was presented. In this context, I'm suggesting that people learn to have a strong negative reaction to the word "feedback," even when they don't know for sure that the feedback will be negative or critical.
2 My PhD advisor, Paul Levy, and I distilled decades of feedback research into this four-part model in our 2015 book, *Using Feedback in Organizational Consulting* (Gregory & Levy, 2015).
3 Back on My Feet is a non-profit operating in 16 US cities that helps individuals experiencing homelessness reinvent their lives through running. Members go through extraordinary personal transformation, and ultimately land in independent housing, with full-time employment.

What Gets in the Way   **2**

In this chapter, we will

- Explore the challenges that arise related to all four elements of a feedback exchange.
- Highlight important nuances that can make or break the success of a feedback exchange.
- Distinguish which aspects of the feedback exchange are under the control of the feedback provider and feedback recipient.

As you saw in Chapter 1, feedback plays a critical role in helping people develop self-awareness, understand their impact on others, gauge their progress to goals, and gather valuable data to learn, grow, and have higher performance. But the stark reality is that many people are so uncomfortable with feedback that they dread and actively avoid giving, asking for, or receiving feedback. Life experiences shape our negative connotation of and attitudes toward feedback. Every feedback exchange—with parents, teachers, coaches, and camp counselors, and later with professors, bosses, colleagues, and partners—shapes our overall attitude toward feedback: our feedback orientation. And yet, chances are that most of the influential individuals in our lives are not highly skilled when it comes to giving and receiving feedback. A lifetime of poorly delivered, thoughtless feedback, provided in the wrong place at the wrong time by people who are uncomfortable providing feedback slowly contributes to our propensity to bristle at the mere mention of the word "feedback." Recent research has

DOI: 10.4324/9781003486510-2

shown that this sense of dread isn't just in our minds—it's also in our bodies. And it's not unique to being on the receiving end of feedback—*providing* feedback can also make people feel just as anxious and uncomfortable. When asked to participate in a feedback exchange following a negotiation, both the recipient and the provider showed increased heart rate (as much as a 50% increase) and higher levels of anxiety (West et al., 2018).

In this chapter, we will take a closer look at what gets in the way of having productive, helpful feedback exchanges, from the lenses of both giving and receiving feedback. We'll frame these challenges using the same four-element model that you learned about in Chapter 1 (Gregory & Levy, 2015). The remaining chapters of the book (Chapters 3–5) offer practical, evidence-based solutions to help you do your very best when it comes to giving, asking for and receiving, and using feedback.

What Gets in the Way: The Feedback Source

Negative experiences with feedback, which shape our ongoing feedback beliefs and attitudes, are largely attributable to the behaviors and choices of feedback providers (the source): what they say (the message); how, when, and where they choose to say it (context); and our (as recipients) relationships with or perceptions of them as individuals. As you saw in Chapter 1, the feedback source is not limited to other people; feedback also comes from technology and our own inner monologue as we assess our experiences throughout the day. However, when it comes to what gets in the way of having effective feedback exchanges, it's other people who introduce the greatest complexities and challenges. In addition to managing the interpersonal dynamics involved in feedback conversations, recipients are also at the mercy of the choices that feedback providers make about the message and their delivery.

We'll get deeper into common pitfalls related to the message and the context shortly. For now, we'll focus on four aspects of the feedback source that can get in the way of effective feedback exchanges: the feedback provider's existing relationship with the feedback recipient, their intentions in giving the feedback, their mindset and attitudes about feedback, and their level of skill when it comes to providing feedback.

The Relationship Between the Feedback Provider and Feedback Recipient

All feedback exchanges take place in the context of an existing relationship, which includes all interactions up until that moment and what will happen in the future. It's not simply a one-time transaction that occurs in a vacuum. As a result, the relationship between the feedback provider and the recipient either helps or harms the feedback exchange. As you saw in Chapter 1, in order for a feedback recipient to be open and accepting of feedback, they must first perceive the feedback provider as trustworthy and credible (Ilgen et al., 1979; Kraus, 2024; Wang et al., 2016). Feedback from an untrustworthy source is likely to be diminished or disregarded by the recipient, as is feedback provided by an individual the recipient considers unknowledgeable about the topic or situation. Feedback from someone the recipient does not trust or perceive as credible may elicit feelings of doubt (*This guy has no idea what he's talking about*), irritation or anger (*Who does she think she is, telling me this—she's completely incompetent!*), or fear (*Are they lying? Are they trying to set me up for failure?*). Whether or not the recipient sees the provider as credible also impacts how they interpret the feedback.

Consider this example: If Theo's manager, Cher, wants to give him some feedback about his performance on a recent project, but Theo does not trust Cher and doesn't think Cher knows what she is talking about regarding this project, Theo will be unlikely to accept and use Cher's feedback. Additionally, if Theo and Cher have a history of tension, mistrust, or disagreement, or they simply do not like each other, Theo is going to be much less likely to accept and use Cher's feedback. As another example, I interviewed Finch, a wealth advisor, about her experience giving feedback to clients. She knows that without an established relationship, trust, or credibility, her feedback lacks impact. Says Finch:

> When I give clients feedback, I have to make it land. I can give them statistics or data, but if our relationship isn't in a healthy place, clients won't hear it or apply it. I can't give the best investment management guidance without knowing and understanding the person, their goals, aspirations, and financial health. In order for my feedback to be heard I have

to build the relationship, so they know that I care, and that my feedback and guidance come from a place of trust and credibility.

Prior interactions influence the expectations and behaviors of both feedback provider and feedback recipient. Feedback delivered unskillfully or unhelpfully can have a negative impact on the quality of the relationship going forward, and it can color future feedback exchanges between the two parties. The hierarchical nature of a relationship also impacts feedback exchanges (Mertens & Schollaert, 2024). For instance, giving upward feedback to a leader or manager can feel intimidating and lead people to hold back on sharing feedback. As a result, the higher someone advances in an organization, the fewer people they can rely on for honest, helpful feedback. Feedback conversations are ultimately very human interactions, steeped in emotion, past experiences between the provider and the recipient, and assumptions and judgments they have of each other. The human nature of these interactions can result in feedback providers holding back on giving feedback because they are uncomfortable or worried about how the other person will respond. They may underestimate the lasting impact of their feedback on their relationship with that individual, or fail to recognize that their *lack* of trust, credibility, or relationship will impact how the recipient hears and interprets their feedback.

The Feedback Provider's Attitudes and Intentions

The success of a feedback exchange starts with the feedback provider's intentions. Remember that feedback is data for the recipient about their behavior, meant to help them become more self-aware, learn, adjust, have higher performance, or make progress on their goals. When a feedback provider's intention is anything *other* than sharing data to help the other person, the conversation is already doomed. For example, in my consulting work related to feedback, I have found that some feedback providers use negative feedback as a means to exert power over or feel superior to the feedback recipient. I have heard things like "I want to put this person in their place," which represents an intention to make the recipient feel small, shamed, or cut down by the feedback provider.

Because feedback takes place in the flow of an existing relationship, the way that feedback providers approach their feedback (what they say, and when, where, and how they say it) inevitably impacts that relationship going forward. By adopting an intention of trying to "teach that person a lesson" or make them feel bad, feedback providers set their conversation up for failure and also harm their relationship. Feedback given with the intent to make the other person feel bad will absolutely get in the way of them hearing and accepting that feedback. When I was conducting research for my dissertation in graduate school, one of the participants didn't like something about the way I presented my study. They reached out to me, my PhD advisor, and the Institutional Review Board (IRB) that oversaw research at my university, saying I "should be cut off at the knees" for the way I was going about my research. This feedback was not objective—there was nothing objectively wrong with my approach and it had been vetted extensively by my dissertation committee and the IRB. To me, this feedback felt like it was intended to harm: to somehow get me in trouble or interfere with my research. The feedback provider offered no useful or constructive information, nor specifics about what they disagreed with. As a result, I wasn't able to actually do anything with their feedback, and the exchange just raised even more questions for me about what this person was seeing or experiencing that was a problem.

Perhaps you have had the experience of working with a manager or peers who provide unconstructive feedback. It's no wonder so many people have weak feedback orientations and actively avoid feedback conversations when past experiences have led them to feel small and singled-out, particularly when that feedback is not specific, evidence-based, or focused on observable behaviors. In short, when feedback providers have *any* intention other than helping the other person, it's likely that the feedback exchange is not going to go well. In my conversations with people about why they held back on sharing feedback, one common response is that the other person "should just know" about their behavior and its impact. If ever you find yourself thinking or saying these same words and therefore holding back on sharing feedback, I encourage you to let go of the belief that they "should just know," because they probably are not aware of the impact of their behavior. You may have identified an important blind spot, and not sharing your feedback takes away an opportunity for the recipient to learn and become more self-aware. When a feedback provider has data or observations that would be useful to another person and holds back on sharing those data or observations, both parties lose out. The feedback recipient misses out on the useful data and opportunity to learn, and the feedback provider probably has to continue living with whatever isn't going well.

The decision to share feedback can also be influenced by our mindset, which underlies our beliefs about people in general. Carol Dweck, an iconic professor and researcher at Stanford University, identified the concepts of *fixed v. growth* mindsets (2006).[1] According to Dweck and her research, individuals who hold a fixed mindset are more likely to believe that people and their abilities are what they are and cannot really change. In contrast, a growth mindset corresponds to the belief that people can learn, grow, and change. You will probably not be surprised to read that individuals who don't believe people can change are less likely to give useful feedback to others, and more likely to focus on the *person* as opposed to their *behavior* when framing their feedback (Heslin et al., 2005; Zhang et al., 2020). In the next section on the feedback message, we'll see why person-focused feedback is less effective and more likely to derail a feedback conversation than behavior-focused feedback.

A feedback provider's attitudes and past experiences with feedback also impact their feedback behavior with others. Fear, discomfort, and underestimating others' interest in feedback are common reasons why someone may hold back on sharing feedback that could be useful to the recipient (Abi-Esber et al., 2022). When we worry about how the recipient might respond to the feedback, or second guess whether we really know what we are talking about, we hold back on giving feedback. As you learned in Chapter 1, each of us has a feedback orientation that encapsulates our attitudes and feelings toward feedback. Many years ago, my PhD advisor and frequent co-author Paul Levy and I did a study looking at the impact of manager feedback orientation on employee perceptions of the feedback environment. Research had consistently shown that *employee* feedback orientation and their perceptions of the feedback environment are highly correlated, so we wanted to know whether a manager's feedback orientation impacted the kind of feedback environment they created at work. Our findings had a surprising result: the manager's attitudes regarding the utility of feedback (a sub-scale of feedback orientation) were *negatively* related to how often they provided negative feedback. In other words, if the manager believes that feedback has a lot of utility, then, according to their employees, they gave negative feedback less often (Gregory & Levy, 2008). What surprised us about this finding is that negative feedback has a lot of utility for helping people learn, grow, have higher performance, and gain self-awareness. So, why would managers who believed in the utility of feedback hold back on sharing such useful data? One possibility is that these managers balance how often they share positive and negative feedback, in order to not overwhelm their direct reports. Or, it is possible that because their negative feedback is provided skillfully, their direct reports don't recognize it as "negative" compared to what they might expect negative feedback to look, sound, and feel like.

Research has also shown that managers with a strong feedback orientation (those who tend to value, use, and seek out feedback for themselves) are more likely to be perceived as better coaches by their direct reports (Steelman & Wolfeld, 2018). While coaching and providing feedback are different skills, they are certainly related, and both pertain to how effective managers are at developing and growing their employees. These researchers also found that managers with a strong feedback orientation who provide coaching, build relationships, and create a favorable feedback environment help to strengthen their employees' feedback orientations. Employees who work with managers who have weak feedback orientations (those who do not tend to value, use, and seek out feedback for themselves) miss out on these benefits. Although there is more research to be done, it is likely that feedback providers who have a weak feedback orientation are less likely to provide frequent, high-quality feedback, thereby letting their own attitudes and beliefs about feedback get in the way of sharing valuable data with others.

The Feedback Provider's Level of Feedback Skill

A feedback provider who simply does not know how to provide feedback effectively will negatively impact the feedback exchange. Here, we start dipping into the nuances of the feedback message, which we'll explore in more detail in the next section. Research has identified attributes of the feedback message that contribute to how the feedback will be received. Feedback providers who lack the knowledge of feedback best practices and the skills to apply them are far less likely to provide feedback that is structured and delivered in a way that will maximize good outcomes, such as the feedback recipient receiving, accepting, understanding, and using the feedback.

In addition to how they structure the message, feedback providers also influence the feedback exchange by how they approach the conversation. Effective feedback conversations are not merely a transaction. Feedback providers who expect to simply deliver the feedback and quickly move on are not setting feedback exchanges up for success. Effective feedback conversations are a dialogue (a concept referred to as "symmetry"), not a monologue or one-way conversation (Anseel & Sherf, 2024; Barry & Crant, 2000). As we'll see when we get into behaviors of the feedback recipient, ideally the feedback recipient asks questions to clarify and ensure they understand the feedback. The likelihood that the feedback is delivered clearly, flawlessly, and with no gaps is slim; feedback providers are remiss to expect that they won't need to answer a few questions.

Over the years, I have also found that feedback providers who are uncomfortable providing feedback resort to a tactic that I call "talking themselves into a hole." Rather than simply *planning what they want to say, saying it, and stop talking,* they keep talking after sharing the core message and therefore leave the feedback recipient confused and unclear about what the crux of the feedback is. The most effective feedback is clear and direct, with minimal pre-amble and post-amble. Additionally, many people have learned throughout their lives or careers to use a method known as the "feedback sandwich," where negative feedback is sandwiched between two pieces of positive feedback in order to "soften the blow."[2] Research does not support the sandwich approach. Rather than easing delivery, the message tends to get lost or misconstrued. Feedback recipients leave the conversation feeling confused—was that good or was it bad?—and unclear on what the real issue is and how they should take action. Worse yet, the more you practice the feedback sandwich, the more people around you will come to expect that any praise will be followed

THE FEEDBACK SANDWICH

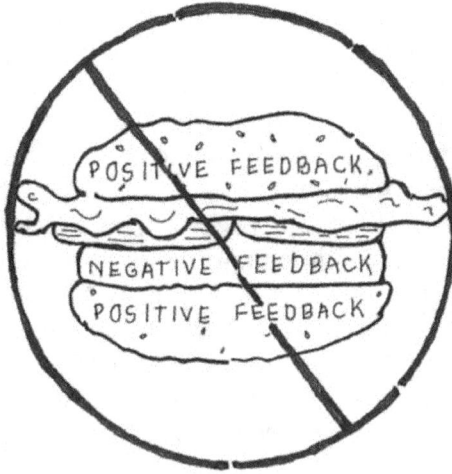

JUST SAY NO

Figure 2.1 Stick to eating sandwiches, not using them to give feedback.

by negative feedback. When stuffed in a feedback sandwich, positive feedback—which is important for building relationships and psychological safety—will instead come across as disingenuous, inauthentic, and a mere sugar coating for the *real* message. As professor and author Brené Brown (2018) says, "Clear is kind, unclear is unkind."

What Gets in the Way: The Message

The feedback provider chooses what they will say and how to frame the feedback message. As you saw in Chapter 1, the words and framing of the message have a significant impact on what the feedback recipient hears and how they react or respond to it. As a result, there are many opportunities for the feedback to land in an ineffective or unhelpful way. We'll focus on three nuances of the feedback message that can make or break the exchange: feedback type, the focus of the feedback, and the extent to which the feedback is evidence-based and specific.

Inappropriate Feedback Type

Because negative feedback highlights a deficit between the current state and the goal or desired state, it can elicit negative emotions, such as disappointment, anxiety, frustration, fear, or demotivation. For example, say you own a restaurant and are hoping for two Michelin Stars this year (your goal). Learning that you are awarded only one Michelin Star—despite being a huge honor—is technically negative feedback because you fell short of reaching your goal of two stars. While many chefs or restauranteurs would be thrilled with the news of receiving a Michelin Star, in this instance you may experience anger, frustration, disappointment, or sadness because you still have a gap between your current state (one star) and your desired state (two stars). This example highlights the importance of feedback *type* and its interaction with feedback sign (positive vs. negative). We introduced the concept of feedback type in Chapter 1; it includes outcome and process feedback. Learning about your Michelin Star award for the year is an example of *outcome* feedback—a final, overall assessment of your performance. Other examples of outcome feedback include an annual performance rating, a final grade in a class, news about whether or not you were selected for the job, and whether you receive the gold medal or the silver medal in the 100-meter dash. It feels evaluative. Contrast this with *process* feedback, which tells you how you are doing as you are working on something, before you reach the final outcome. Process feedback feels more developmental and conducive to helping people adjust their behavior in order to achieve their goals; it is given "along the way" and therefore lends itself to being incorporated into our work and efforts. Receiving only outcome feedback can be unhelpful and demoralizing. If we don't know how we are doing along the way (e.g., if we don't receive process feedback), and then find out at the end of our efforts that we have missed our target, a sense of failure and demotivation is common. At that point, it's too late to do something with the feedback, and all we know is that we didn't achieve what we'd been striving for, despite our best efforts. Specific process feedback enables feedback recipients to act with agility and course-correct their behavior before it's too late.

In school, feedback from your professor delivered throughout the term, such as grades on assignments, can be considered process feedback leading up to your final grade, which constitutes outcome feedback. At work, process feedback includes day-to-day feedback from your manager, customers, or colleagues. Your annual performance rating and review are akin to outcome feedback, since it presumably occurs at the end of the performance period, providing an overall evaluation of performance during the year. In recent years, many organizations have adopted performance management processes that encourage quarterly check-ins or conversations between managers and employees—these could be considered process feedback. These are generally non-evaluative, whereas that feeling of being evaluated, such as your annual year-end review, is a hallmark of outcome feedback. Crossing feedback type (outcome vs. process) with feedback sign (positive vs. negative) results in four distinct combinations, which, in turn, evoke very different responses from the recipient (Medvedeff et al., 2008; see Figure 2.2). Not surprisingly, people like positive outcome feedback: it tells them they have succeeded and did a good job at whatever they were working on. What may surprise you is that the next most popular type of feedback—which leads people to actually ask for *more* subsequent feedback—is negative process feedback. Negative process feedback is feedback along the way that tells you where you are off—such as what you need to do more of, less of, or differently in order to achieve your goals. Herein lies one of my favorite findings of all time about feedback. People don't hate negative feedback; they just dislike negative *outcome* feedback, which essentially tells them they failed at whatever they were doing.

FEEDBACK TYPE	FEEDBACK SIGN	
	POSITIVE	NEGATIVE
PROCESS	FEELS GOOD; LIMITED VALUE, TELLS PEOPLE THEY ARE ON THE RIGHT TRACK TO MEET THEIR GOALS. TOO MUCH CAN RESULT IN SLOWING DOWN THEIR EFFORTS OVER TIME (COASTING).	GREATEST INFORMATIONAL VALUE! TELLS SOMEONE THEY ARE OFF ON THEIR GOALS, AND ALSO HOW TO GET BACK ON TRACK.
OUTCOME	FEELS GREAT! TELLS SOMEONE THEY MET THEIR GOAL OR HAD HIGH PERFORMANCE AT THE CONCLUSION OF A TASK, AND NOW THEY'RE DONE.	DEMOTIVATING. TELLS SOMEONE THEY DIDN'T MEET THEIR GOAL OR DELIVER HIGH PERFORMANCE AND THE TASK IS NOW COMPLETE. TOO LATE TO MAKE CHANGES.

Figure 2.2 Crossing feedback sign with feedback type results in four very different types of feedback, some more effective for influencing behavior than others.

For example, when I interviewed Alex, the general manager of an actual (not the theoretical example above) Michelin-starred restaurant, she shared her frustration about unhappy guests providing only negative outcome feedback.

> When guests tell us at the end of the night—or even later after they have left the restaurant—that they had a bad experience or didn't like something, there is no opportunity to repair the situation. We have set up so many opportunities—in fact, 10 specific opportunities—throughout the meal for guests to provide feedback.

Alex's frustration is understandable. The ten opportunities she and her team have created for guests to provide feedback on their dining experience is classic process feedback. Staff at the restaurant ask guests for feedback on their food after every course. If staff members notice an unfinished dish or a drink pushed aside, they ask guests specifically for feedback on that item and offer something different on the house if the guest was disappointed or unsatisfied. Dining guests receive comment cards with their bill. They are asked about their overall experience by staff at the end of the meal. Shortly after dining they receive an online rating form (using a 5-point scale plus ratings on specific dimensions and open-ended comments) via email or a reservation app. If guests are unhappy with some aspect of their experience, letting the staff know in the moment enables them to course-correct and fix the situation to delight the customers and achieve their shared goal of having a wonderful dining experience. Sharing only negative outcome feedback is fruitless, because the experience has ended and it's too late for the staff to take action.

Because it arrives only after a project or experience has ended, negative outcome feedback is likely to result in negative emotional reactions and a drop in motivation. Positive outcome feedback, however, leaves people feeling satisfied and justified in their efforts because they learn that their work has paid off. In an ideal world, we would all receive specific, negative process feedback that is easy to apply and ultimately results in receiving positive outcome feedback when we meet our goal. But that's not always realistic, and negative outcome feedback is bound to occur at some point in everyone's life. One adaptive way feedback recipients can reframe uninspiring negative outcome feedback is to expand the time horizon and context, and view outcome feedback as a form of process feedback. For example, if you received a negative annual performance review you can look at that review as the outcome evaluation: I failed. Alternatively, you can look at the 30-year trajectory of your career and see this annual review as one milestone along the way. Interpreting that negative review as feedback to help you have a better year next year is actually a way to reframe what feels like outcome feedback into process feedback. For example, Goodloe, a professional artist, shared with me that he sees feedback he receives on his art as input to his ongoing approach to creating.

> Getting only positive feedback can be stifling if it makes me complacent and stop striving to change or evolve what I'm doing. Negative feedback, even if it makes me doubt what I'm doing, there's no way I can say it's a bad thing. And knowing that whatever I am working on is not over allows me to incorporate feedback into what I do next. Having that perspective in the back of my mind allows me to incorporate any feedback that I get into my work.

People want, value, and appreciate negative process feedback because it provides a roadmap for how they need to change their behavior to improve. It can be put into practice right away, as people are still working on their project or task and help them move closer to their goal. Feedback can go wrong when feedback providers focus disproportionately on giving negative outcome feedback or positive process feedback. Positive process feedback tells the recipient, "You're doing fine, keep going," which is helpful and important for them to see that their efforts are on track and moving them toward their goal. It is motivating and reinforces their behavior. And, research has shown that when people continue receiving positive process feedback about the same task, after a while they basically tune it out and stop looking for more feedback (Medvedeff et al., 2008). One unfortunate pattern that I see frequently in organizations is employees primarily receiving positive process feedback throughout the year, only to be surprised with negative outcome feedback in a year-end review. I often hear stories from workshop participants and students about being surprised at the end of the year with negative feedback that they had never heard before, even if the behavior or situation took place weeks or months earlier. This situation leads them to wonder, "Why didn't you tell me this sooner?" Here we see the role of the feedback provider and context come into play. Why did the feedback provider wait until the year-end review to share the feedback? Did their discomfort sharing the feedback lead them to avoid and delay the conversation? We will see in our section on context that waiting too long to share feedback is more likely to elicit negative emotions from the recipient. But first, let's look at another critical failure point in the framing of the message: focusing on the person rather than their behavior.

Focused on the Person Rather Than Their Behavior

The focal point of the feedback plays an enormous role in how it lands with the recipient. Person-focused feedback speaks to the recipient's personality, character, abilities, or who they are as a person, whereas behavior-focused feedback addresses some action they took, or something they did or did not do. Recall that the reason we give feedback is to influence future behavior. It is really hard to change your abilities or who you are as a person; changing our future actions and behaviors is much easier in contrast. So, you will not be shocked to learn that person-focused feedback is less likely to be received well compared with behavior-focused feedback. In particular, negative feedback that focuses on the *person*, rather than that person's *behavior*, is significantly more likely to elicit a defensive reaction. For example, saying "Noor, you are not a good public speaker" is much more likely to make Noor defensive than "Noor, your speech today lacked structure, and your voice was quiet, so it was hard to follow." The person-focused example focuses on Noor as a person, whereas the behavior-focused example focuses on Noor's actions—her observable behavior. Receiving feedback that focuses on you as a person feels more critical, sometimes like a judgment or character attack. It provokes feelings of self-consciousness and draws attention inward, away from the task at hand. Person-focused feedback also feels more like an opinion, rather than an evidence-based assessment. Not only is person-focused feedback hard to accept, it's also not very helpful. Behavior change is challenging, but it's much easier than attempting to change who you are as a person. In the example of Noor, the person-focused feedback is general and gives her little insight into what about her speech was ineffective. The behavior-focused feedback is more likely to enable Noor to do better next time—to give her speech more structure and to speak up.

It's easy to assume that person-focused feedback is only counterproductive when it is negative. Praising someone for who they are as a person feels generous; we want them to know how great they are as a person, right? Wrong! Though it may seem counterintuitive, Carol Dweck's (2006) groundbreaking research found that person-focused (as opposed to behavior-focused) praise can render people less resilient to future failures. For example, if a child gets an "A" on a test, it's tempting to say "Quentin, you got an A on your test! You are so smart!" After repeated instances of Quentin hearing how smart he is after he gets good grades, he learns to associate his success with his abilities. So, one day when Quentin fails an exam in college, he starts to believe he's not smart and that he doesn't have what it takes to succeed. Just as he always attributed his successes to his abilities, now he's attributing his *lack* of success to his *lack* of ability. Instead, if Quentin had repeatedly been praised for his hard work and preparation, he would have learned to attribute his success to his efforts, rather than his abilities. Therefore, when he fails a test during his first year in college, he will attribute his failure to missing class and insufficient studying and preparation, rather than his lack of intelligence. Behavior-focused feedback—both positive and negative—empowers us to see a connection between our efforts and outcomes, enabling a growth mindset, a stronger sense of self-efficacy, and a belief that we can change our behavior to attain the outcomes that we want. Person-focused feedback, however, conditions us to believe that our abilities determine our successes and failures and that those abilities are fixed. People with a fixed mindset believe that whether they fail or succeed, it's because of who they are and the hand they were dealt (Dweck, 2006).

Giving person-focused feedback can have an adverse impact on both short- and long-term outcomes. In the short term, person-focused feedback makes people defensive, less likely to accept the feedback, and less likely to actually do something with the feedback. In the long term, it can cultivate a maladaptive fixed mindset that holds people back from changing their behavior or increasing their effort to achieve desired outcomes. Person-focused feedback is less conducive to the recipient taking action and more likely to result in an uncomfortable, emotionally charged conversation that leaves the recipient feeling confused, offended, self-conscious, or ready to push back and engage in debate. Rather than taking the person-focused feedback as data to inform their future behavior, the recipient may be prepared to defend what they believe to be true about them, resulting in a wasted opportunity to learn and probably a damaged relationship.

Not Evidence-Based and Specific

By this point you know that we want feedback to provide clear, informative, useful data that will enable the recipient to learn, adjust their behavior, or become more self-aware. And the more evidence-based and specific the feedback is, the more likely that is to happen. Feedback providers often botch a feedback exchange when they are vague, speak in generalities, focus on opinions rather than facts, and make inferences or assumptions about why someone did something. The most useful feedback focuses only on observable behaviors, things that you could see with your own eyes or capture on camera or with metrics. Many feedback providers get themselves into trouble by going a few steps beyond the observable behaviors and including assumptions about why the recipient did what they did, or what they were thinking. For example, truly evidence-based feedback might sound something like "Jin, you were 15 minutes late to our last three weekly team meetings." Full stop, that's it. Poorly constructed feedback sounds more like "Jin, you are always late to meetings. I know you don't think they are very important, but the rest of the team wants to see you there." What's wrong with that feedback? It is a generalization—"you are always late"—rather than specific and evidence based. Contrast this with the first example—"you were 15 minutes late to our last three team meetings." To the untrained eye (or ear), these two statements probably don't seem that different. But when considered in the light of the feedback goals we've discussed, it's clear that the first, more specific example tells Jin exactly what he did and when. It's something that could be captured on camera, if there was a camera in the team meeting. It includes no judgments or assumptions about why Jin was late. That latter example does not include specific evidence and is therefore more likely to result in Jin defending himself, arguing, "No, I am not always late. I have had scheduling conflicts with the last three meetings but before that I was always on time." The latter example also includes some assumptions about what is happening in Jin's brain. The temptation to psychoanalyze can be a pitfall for feedback providers. As much as we may think we know why people do what they do or what they are thinking, unless we can see inside their brains we really don't know. Our assumptions are inherently biased by our own beliefs, experiences, and expectations, which are not the same as anyone else's (this is why advice is flawed—it, too, is inherently biased by our per-spective). Adding that second sentence to the feedback, "I know you don't think they are very important . . .," is another way to ensure that Jin focuses on defending himself, rather than engaging in a constructive dialogue about the real issue: being late to team meetings.

The more specific the feedback is, the easier it is for the recipient to understand what they did, when, and where. Specific feedback is also much easier to take action on and turn into behavior change. Behavior change is hard, and more specific feedback is easier to convert into small steps to start moving in the right direction. In our example with Jin, the vague example does not even specify which meetings: "you are always late to meetings." Because our better example notes that he has been "15 minutes late to the last three team meetings," Jin can identify what caused him to be 15 minutes late to those specific meetings. This may also lead to a helpful dialogue, in which Jin shares with the feed-back provider what is getting in the way of him being on time, and the two can work together to find a solution. The vague example, instead, is likely to prompt Jin to debate the feedback and defend himself.

Think about feedback you have received recently. Was it evidence-based? Did it focus on something you could see with your eyes or capture on camera? Or was it a vague generalization or opinion? How specific was it? Did it help you better understand what you are doing or not doing, when and where? Feedback providers often shortchange their message by leaving out useful detail and framing their feedback around generalizations or inferences. Instead, consider "what exactly did this person do or not do, when, and where?" Notice that I left out the "why," because we don't know why the person did what they did. Making assumptions about the why will likely only derail your feedback conversation.

Not Clear and Direct

Finally, feedback providers do a disservice to themselves and the person they are providing feedback to when their message is not clear and direct. At the end of our section on the source, we mentioned Brené Brown's quote, "Clear is kind, unclear is unkind." Providing a convoluted or indirect message leaves the feedback recipient with the task of trying to decode or figure out the issue, which is unhelpful to them and creates enormous opportunity for assumptions and misunderstandings. In my work over the years, I have consistently been surprised by how infrequently people pause to think about or write down what they want to say. They walk into challenging negative feedback conversations and "shoot from the hip," saying whatever comes to mind in the moment and hope it comes out right. Not preparing for the conversation by figuring out how to share data and observations in the clearest and most straightforward way possible when constructing the message is yet another way that feedback providers impede the success of their feedback exchanges. In the next section we will explore challenges that can arise in context—when and how feedback is provided—another element in the feedback exchange that is heavily influenced by the feedback provider.

What Gets in the Way: Context

The context in which feedback is provided plays an important role in how the feedback recipient hears and reacts to feedback, and feedback providers have a lot of choice when it comes to selecting the right (or wrong) context. Common pitfalls include waiting too long to give feedback, providing feedback in public rather than in private, and choosing an ineffective medium.

Waiting Too Long to Provide Feedback

If the purpose of providing feedback is to help the recipient course correct or make changes in their behaviors, then giving it as soon as possible allows them to take action right away rather than continue doing something that might not be working very well. This is one of several reasons why feedback is best provided promptly. Providing feedback soon after something transpires also ensures the situation is fresh in the provider's mind, so they can share the information clearly and accurately. Research has shown that when feedback is shared in a timely manner, the recipient is more likely to pay attention and retain the feedback (van der Kleij et al., 2012). The situation will also be fresh in their mind, so they, too, can recall what they did or did not do. In other words, prompt feedback provides higher-quality, more specific data. It also shows the recipient that the feedback provider cares. Waiting too long to provide negative feedback can evoke feelings of frustration, anger, and apathy and reduce the likelihood that the recipient will accurately remember what happened in the first place. Long delays send a message that the feedback provider doesn't really care or that it wasn't a priority.

Unfortunately, holding on to useful feedback for days, weeks, or months is not unusual for many feedback providers. Often, when people have feedback, they delay giving it because they are uncomfortable having what feels like a challenging conversation, so they avoid or procrastinate. Perhaps the feedback provider thinks, "Let me wait and see what happens; maybe they will figure it out on their own" (they probably won't), or "I am not confident I know what I'm talking about or that I'm the right person to say something" (you probably are). Although these delay tactics might seem well-intentioned, waiting often results in feedback that is never shared or is shared so late that the recipient feels demoralized or frustrated that the moment to address the behavior has already passed. When a person has useful data or observations that could help their colleague, friend, or family member, and they choose to sit on it rather than muster the courage to share it, they are priori-tizing their own comfort over helping the other person and taking away an opportunity for that person to learn and improve. When a manager saves up feedback for a several months to share during a formal performance review, they do a disservice to themselves, the feedback recipient, and the entire organization. Hearing some-thing for the first time in an annual performance review is sur-prising, overwhelming, and frustrating for the recipient. Instead, if that manager shared feedback earlier in the year right after they observed a behavior, their employee would have been able to do something with it sooner. The feedback would have been easier to process and accept; now, at the end of the year the recipient is probably thinking, "Why didn't you tell me this sooner?" It sends a message that their manager either didn't care enough to say any-thing at the time or they are cowardly or untrustworthy. Delaying feedback also risks compromising the quality of the feedback. By sharing feedback at the end of the year, rather than promptly after the behavior, it's likely that either the manager or the recipient, or both, will not clearly and accurately remember what actually happened in the moment. The feedback may be less specific or feel unfair and lead to a debate if the two parties recall the situation differently. These timeliness considerations apply to positive feed-back just as much as negative feedback.

There are two exceptions for the practice of providing timely feedback: situations that are emotionally charged or public settings (discussed in the next section). Feedback providers can get them-selves into challenging situations when they provide feedback too soon after the event, if either they or the feedback recipient is emotionally activated, such as feeling angry, sad, or even joyful (London & Smither, 2002). For example, if Pedro and Julia just came out of a really bad client meeting where Pedro said some-thing that made the client angry and the conversation devolved into an argument, Julia would probably not help the situation by providing Pedro with negative feedback on his behavior immedi-ately after the client leaves the room. If he's angry and emotionally hijacked, Pedro likely will not hear and process the feedback and may instead simply react and direct his anger toward Julia. By waiting a few hours or even days later to share her feedback, Julia may increase the likelihood that Pedro will be in the right frame of mind to listen and hear her feedback. By sharing the feedback too soon, Julia would waste her opportunity, and the situation could escalate further.

Let's flip this around and assume the conversation with the client was full of fabulous surprises and Pedro is overcome with positive emotions about their success. If Julia wanted to share substantive positive feedback with Pedro about his role in the meeting, he might not really hear and mindfully process her positive feedback if he is experiencing intense positive emotions. Yes, strong positive emotions can also get in the way of really hearing the feedback. So, again, waiting a few hours or days to share specific, positive feedback may result in a more meaningful conversation. Similarly, if Julia chose to share her feedback to Pedro in front of the client and the rest of the team, Pedro would also be less likely to receive it well than if Julia waited to share the feedback in private. Let's continue to pull this thread and examine why feedback given in public can derail a conversation.

Providing Feedback in Public

Most people deeply dislike receiving feedback in front of other people—particularly negative feedback—and research has consistently shown that a public setting impacts how people hear and react to the feedback (Ashford & Northcraft, 1992; Levy et al., 1995; Westerman & Westerman, 2013). Perhaps the only thing worse than feeling criticized is being criticized in front of your peers, colleagues, classmates, or even random strangers. I once had the troubling experience of hearing a team leader loudly provide detailed negative feedback to one of her team members in the middle of an office kitchen during lunch, for all to hear. The team member looked mortified, and I'm willing to bet he was so focused on his own discomfort that he didn't absorb much of the feedback. Several studies have examined the impact of publicly provided feedback on recipients' feelings of *public self-consciousness*, which is the tendency to focus inwardly on the self and the feeling of being observed by others who are present (Levy et al., 1995). Because most people want to present the best version of themselves, receiving negative feedback in the presence of others can feel threatening and anxiety-provoking. Both anxiety and elevated feelings of self-consciousness have been linked to cognitive failures

(Matthews & Wells, 1988; Wells & Matthews, 1994), such as diminished perception, attention, and memory. In other words, if you choose to give someone feedback in front of other people, this will activate in them feelings of self-consciousness and anxiety, which will impact their ability to pay attention to, hear, and process your feedback. They may also leave the interaction with feelings of discomfort, which may harm future interactions that you have with them. A quote, often attributed to author and poet Maya Angelou, captures what really matters: "People will forget what you said, forget what you did, but they will never forget how you made them feel."

What's more, research has consistently shown that people are significantly less likely to actively seek additional feedback when they are in public, compared to when they are in private settings (Ashford & Northcraft, 1992; Kraus, 2024; Levy et al., 1995). In other words, if you want the recipient to ask questions and engage in a dialogue, use a private setting for the feedback exchange. This tendency pertains to both negative *and* positive feedback. Some managers are quick to assume that people love being praised in front of others at work, but that is simply not a universal truth. In fact, one study found that people perceived both positive and negative feedback provided publicly as less just (less fair) than privately shared feedback (Westerman & Westerman, 2013). Another study found that private feedback was more likely to boost motivation than public praise (Delavallade, 2021). Praise or positive feedback delivered in public can also activate feelings of self-consciousness and anxiety, just like negative feedback can. Providing positive feedback publicly therefore can interfere with how well the recipient hears and processes the feedback and also waste an opportunity for the feedback provider to create a meaningful moment and invest in their relationship with the recipient, which is more likely to occur when the feedback is provided privately. Research has also shown that both the feedback recipient and provider can be seen negatively by observers when positive feedback is provided in public (Chan & Sengupta, 2013); the feedback may be seen as flattery or disingenuous. It also alienates the other people in the room. Imagine praising one person in a group and saying nothing to the others; your lack of feedback to them may easily stir up feelings of discomfort and self-doubt.

Technology has blurred the lines between private and public feedback. The other day I received an email from an online clothing store where I had recently purchased a few items. The email caught my eye because of an "invitation to provide feedback on your purchase." As you can imagine I perk up anytime I see the word "feedback," and immediately clicked on the email. I expected to find a short online survey where I would provide input on the quality of the products I had purchased, or perhaps on the shopping experience. Instead, I found that the link took me to an online review platform, where I was asked to write an open-ended review that would be posted publicly on their website. I paused to consider how feedback in the digital age has taken on a new form, where consumers are able to provide indirect feedback that can meaningfully influence other consumers' choices, often without sharing their feedback directly with the business. Let's take a look now at the impact of the feedback medium.

Choosing an Ineffective Medium

Feedback providers have many choices for how to deliver feedback, such as in-person conversations, phone calls, video calls, email, text, Slack or instant message, written comments in a document, and more. Social media, smartphones, and wearable technology have added a layer of complexity and immediacy to how we give, receive, and use feedback. Technology increases the speed and availability of feedback, which can be helpful at times, and also encroaches on the precious time needed for mindful processing when recipients feel an urgency to respond right away. The problem with texts and instant messages is that the provider doesn't always know where the person on the other end is or what they are doing. Receiving negative feedback via text message when you are in the middle of something and not expecting it can be deeply distracting and off-putting. Not only does it disrupt whatever you are currently working on, it also diminishes the impact of the feedback, as you will be more likely to disregard it, have a negative reaction to it, or dismiss it altogether. Text- or email-based feedback also requires the recipient to infer tone or emotion, often leading to a misinterpretation of the meaning and intent of an otherwise innocuous message. For example, a text or email that simply reads "That's fine" might be interpreted differently depending on the sender or the context. It might feel terse or passive aggressive in some situations, or straightforward and appropriate in others. Without hearing tone or seeing facial expressions, we lack some of the color that helps us interpret the words.

In addition to texting, cell phones enable feedback conversations to take place anytime, anyplace. This can be helpful for sharing timely feedback, but it also introduces complexity because the feedback provider and recipient may be in very different settings and frames of mind, which can lead to an unproductive and potentially harmful conversation. For instance, an individual working for a multinational company could receive a phone call from a colleague in another time zone early in the morning, late at night, or while having dinner with their family or attending a child's basketball game. Mateo, a vice president in a large global organization, recounted to me a story about answering a work call on a Friday evening while celebrating a family birthday. The caller, his colleague from the US west coast, provided some tough feedback on a meeting they had earlier that week. Mateo was not in the physical or mental place to have a conversation like this, and as a result became defensive. The poorly timed negative feedback impacted his mood, which had a spill-over effect to his family and the rest of the weekend. In hindsight, both Mateo and his colleague (the caller) were in the wrong. His colleague was trying to be efficient and "check a box" by getting the feedback conversation over with but failed to consider what was happening in Mateo's day or take time zones into account. A more effective course of action would have been to put time on the calendar for the following Monday and have the conversation when they were both in the right setting and mindset to have a productive feedback discussion. Mateo, too, could have handled the situation more effectively. He shared with me that he is prone to the unhealthy belief that "feedback happens to me," rather than seeing himself as an equal participant in the feedback conversation. If he could replay this experience all over again, he would have either (a) not answered the call or (b) told his colleague that now wasn't the right time to have this conversation, let's talk on Monday.

One challenge with fast technology, like emails and messaging, is that firing off a quick note is very easy and doesn't require deep thought and planning. Feedback providers who don't pause to consider where the recipient might be or what they are doing, if it's really so urgent that they need to send the message right now, or how the tone of their message could be misconstrued are not setting the feedback conversation up for success. Both texting and emails can be useful for providing feedback, but only under certain circumstances, which we'll explore further in Chapter 3. Technology also allows for what I call "a feedback triangle," which includes the feedback provider, the focus of the feedback (whether a person or a business), and an audience, such as people reading online reviews (see Figure 2.3). Way back in 1995, online auction site eBay introduced a feature that created a fundamental shift in the way consumers interact with businesses. eBay's simple feedback system, which allowed buyers and sellers to rate each other and leave brief comments, enabled never-before-seen transparency between buyers and sellers and is credited with driving eBay's success compared to competitors (Tadelis, 2016). This simple and transparent feedback system is now a standard feature on online commerce sites.

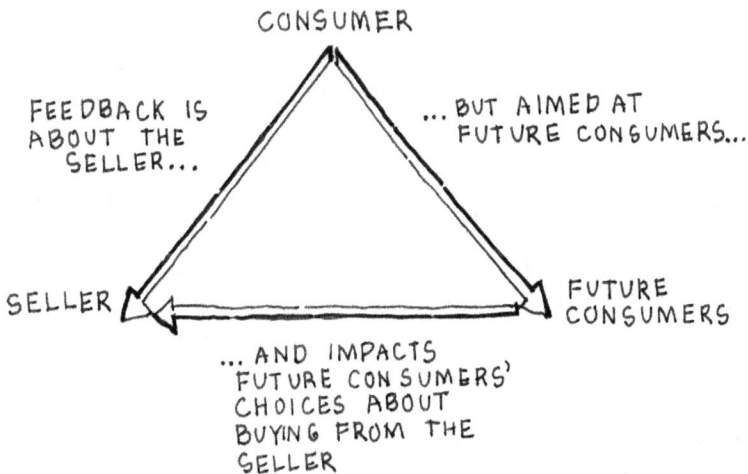

CONSUMER

FEEDBACK IS ABOUT THE SELLER...

...BUT AIMED AT FUTURE CONSUMERS...

SELLER

FUTURE CONSUMERS

...AND IMPACTS FUTURE CONSUMERS' CHOICES ABOUT BUYING FROM THE SELLER

Figure 2.3 Indirect feedback via technology creates a complex communication triangle.

These transparent rating systems, now ubiquitous in online commerce, are valuable to consumers looking to make an informed purchase or have a desirable experience. But this public, indirect feedback triangle is often at odds with the value of timely, direct feedback. Sure, businesses can identify patterns of failure or opportunities that surface through publicly posted customer feedback over time, but the indirect and sometimes delayed nature of feedback on platforms like Yelp prevents businesses from taking immediate action. Online reviews constitute outcome feedback; they provide a summary view of what an experience was like and leave no window to address the feedback and course correct. Research by Cabral and Hortacsu (2010) found that after their first bad review, online auction sellers experience a 13% drop in sales. Similarly, Luca (2016) found that each additional star in a Yelp rating (a 1- to 5-star scale) equates to a 5–9% increase in revenue. According to Yelp's website, 2.5 million unique visitors use the site *each day* to leverage or post one of over 300 million reviews (Yelp, 2025a; 2025b). Users feel a sense of anonymity when providing online feedback, and anonymity often leads to more candid (and sometimes less skillful) feedback (we see this often in 360 feedback; Bracken et al., 2001). Despite opportunities to provide direct feedback in dining or shopping situations, consumers who are uncomfortable providing feedback may gravitate toward the indirect feedback option.

What Gets in the Way: The Recipient

Our discussion of the first three elements of feedback exchanges focused heavily on characteristics, actions, and decisions of the feedback provider. As a result, it's easy to see feedback as "happening to" the recipient, as if the recipient plays a small and passive role in the feedback exchange or is even a "victim" of the feedback. But just as feedback providers can choose the optimal context and content of the feedback exchange, feedback recipients can *choose* to take a more active role in the dialogue and see themselves as an equal participant in the conversation. In this section, we examine several places where feedback exchanges go sour because of some attribute or action of the feedback recipient, including the impact of powerful emotions and unhelpful mindsets, a weak feedback orientation, not listening, taking feedback at face value and not asking questions, and expecting to process the feedback instantaneously.

Not Managing Their Emotions or Mindset

Uncomfortable feedback exchanges can evoke the same biological response as tangible threats, such as encountering a bear on a hike or a creepy person while we are walking home alone at night. The same parts of the brain are engaged in these real and hypothetical threats, and—when activated—they prompt us to fight, flee, or freeze. Because our brains are quick and efficient information-processors with a bias for survival, we learn to anticipate this type of impulsive response when faced with a potential threat. For most people, feedback also elicits this threat response, resulting in a strong, immediate emotional reaction, which can impede our ability to mindfully process the feedback. The ability to mindfully process feedback—to think about it clearly and rationally—is a precursor to accepting and using that feedback (London & Smither, 2002), and can be stifled by powerful emotions, which unfold rapidly. Emotions provide important data to help us assess the safety or threat of a situation, which in turn impacts how we think and make decisions, with positive emotion corresponding to open, expansive cognition, and negative emotions narrowing our thinking (Elfenbein, 2023; Thoebes, 2024). In the face of feedback that feels critical, inaccurate, or personal, an instant emotional reaction may lead to feelings of defensiveness and rejection of the feedback before the recipient has even had time to pause and think about it. A recipient's experience of strong emotions in the moment may present as shutting down and disengaging from the conversation, interrupting or pushing back on the feedback provider in an unconstructive way, or getting so swept up in an emotional reaction that they spiral and don't actually hear and absorb what the feedback provider is saying. Feedback exchanges can go haywire at this point—turning into a cascade of emotionally charged, fear-based responses from both feedback recipient and feedback provider. Failing to give the feedback recipient time and space to process the feedback is a major failure point for feedback providers. "Cool cognition" needs time to catch up with "hot emotion" (this is why we count to 10 when we are angry—to give rational thought some time to catch up), and when the feedback recipient does not have time to step back, let the initial emotional reaction pass, and actually process the feedback, the message often gets lost.

Humans have choice about what they do with powerful emotions, but this requires learning how to notice the emotions, being willing and able to pause before reacting, and intentionally *choosing* a helpful response. Feedback recipients have a responsibility to self-manage in the moment, to notice what is going on in their mind and body and take the necessary steps to stay present in the conversation. This could include saying, "I notice I am having a strong emotional reaction to this feedback. Do you mind if I take some time to process it and we resume our conversation later?" Research has shown that practicing mindfulness in the moment can help feedback recipients manage those emotions, something we'll see more about in Chapter 4 (Thoebes, 2024).

Earlier in this chapter, we touched on the concept of growth versus fixed mindset. A fixed or growth mindset tends to be deeply ingrained but can evolve with time and effort. However, we also have mindsets that represent temporary perspectives that influence how we see and interpret our day-to-day experiences, similar to an attitude. Think of the fixed/growth mindset as your eyesight, whereas mindsets that you temporarily adopt (attitudes) are more like glasses that you can take on and off. These temporary mindsets color our perceptions and the way we experience any situation and interaction and also how we manage our emotions in the moment. The most incredible thing about temporary mindsets is that we can intentionally *choose* them. And often we don't. We let whatever mood, emotions, or thoughts we are currently experiencing automatically slot in without pausing to consider which mindset will best serve us and our goals.

For example, going into a feedback conversation, someone might choose a mindset of courage, curiosity, or collaboration (seeing both participants as being on the same team). As noted previously, feedback recipients often adopt a victim mindset, approaching feedback as something that is happening *to* them. Contrast this with a collaborative mindset, where the recipient is an equal participant in the conversation, more inclined to ask questions and really seek to understand the feedback and own what they decide to do with it. When feedback recipients adopt mindsets of being a victim, a passive participant in the conversation, that the feedback is happening to them, that the feedback provider is right and you simply have to take their feedback, *or* that their feedback provider is a jerk who is out to get them, doesn't know what they are talking about, or has devious intentions, the feedback conversation is not going to be a productive, collaborative dialogue. Certainly, the mindsets, actions, and behaviors of the feedback provider play a role here, but the feedback recipient has full autonomy over what mindset they want to bring to the conversation. Their mindset colors how they hear and perceive the feedback, how they engage in the conversation and handle their emotions, and ultimately what they do (or don't do) with the feedback. And these mindsets are also tied to the feedback recipient's feedback orientation.

Having a Weak Feedback Orientation

Recall that feedback orientation is your attitude toward feedback: if you like it, value it, see utility in it, actively seek it out, and feel inclined to do something with it (Linderbaum & Levy, 2010). Our feedback orientation is shaped over time by our experiences with feedback—the interactions we have with teachers, coaches, bosses, parents, colleagues—and also the feedback cultures where we live and work. Individuals with a weak feedback orientation (which is often coupled with low self-esteem or low self-confidence) tend to be less resilient to and more adversely affected by a low-quality feedback experience, whereas individuals with a strong feedback orientation are likely to be more resilient to and take ownership for a mediocre feedback experience (Northcraft & Ashford, 1990; McCauley et al., 1989).

Feedback orientation has been linked to the likelihood that someone will actively seek feedback, to the quality of the relationship they have with their leader or manager, and to their manager's ratings of their performance (Dahling et al., 2012;

Rasheed et al., 2015). Someone with a weak feedback orientation is unlikely to actively seek out feedback, and more likely to both avoid situations where they receive feedback and have lower-quality relationships with their managers who, in turn, have worse perceptions of their performance. And, unfortunately, poor feedback experiences further reinforce a weak feedback orientation. Failing to proactively ask for feedback isn't limited to people with a weak feedback orientation. Some people don't ask for feedback simply because it doesn't occur to them that they can choose who to ask, about what, where, and when. One of my favorite studies of the past decade, which I briefly mentioned at the start of the chapter, showed that proactively asking for feedback makes the exchange less stressful for both the giver and the receiver (West et al., 2018). These researchers found that giving unsolicited feedback resulted in higher anxiety and heart rate for both parties. However, when control over the feedback exchange was placed in the hands of the recipient and feedback was only provided when the recipient asked for it, both giver and receiver experienced less stress, a lower heart rate, and a friendlier feedback exchange. When people don't proactively ask for feedback, they are choosing to be in feedback exchanges that are more stressful for them and for the person giving the feedback. They are choosing to be at the mercy of others deciding when, how, and about what to give feedback.

Not Listening

Another failure point for feedback recipients is not really listening to the feedback that is being shared. Too often, feedback recipients are more focused on what they will say next or how they will push back on or debate what is being shared, or they are merely caught up in their own inner monologue during the conversation—judging the feedback that is being shared (or the feedback provider as they are speaking) or swirling in feelings of self-consciousness and self-doubt about their performance or abilities. Truly listening requires not only hearing but also giving one's full, undivided attention. Even if a feedback provider is doing a suboptimal job of providing feedback, there is likely some valuable data in there. The only way to fully grasp what the feedback provider is trying to share is to really listen and seek to understand. This means paying close attention to the feedback provider's words and picking up on subtle non-verbal cues, such as their facial expressions or body language, which include important additional data. It also requires quieting the mind and inner monologue as it starts to spin up with reactions, judgments, and fears, all of which get in the way of really listening.

The act of really listening with our full attention not only aids the recipient's comprehension of the feedback but it also plays a role in the dynamic and relationship they have with the provider. Really listening builds trust and psychological safety and failing to do so can chip away at those dynamics. One of my favorite feedback researchers, Manuel London, and his colleagues note that if the recipient appears distracted or shows visible signs that they are doubting or disagree with the feedback, it can cause the feedback provider to detach and worry about the recipient's willingness to participate in the conversation (London et al., 2023). They mention the concept of *perceived listening*, which encompasses the speaker's (feedback provider) perception that the other person is really listening, paying attention, and understanding what they are sharing. When feedback recipients dedicate attention and cognitive resources to planning how they will respond or get swept up in their own feelings of self-consciousness, they are not really listening. Not only do they miss parts of the message, they also provide non-verbal cues to their feedback provider that they aren't really listening, which has the potential to further damage the feedback exchange and harm the relationship between provider and recipient.

In addition to listening during a conversation, feedback requires our full attention and willingness to seek to understand it, regardless of format. Feedback received in an email, from comments on a document, or even (ugh) via text message is easy to scan and gloss over, which is a great way to misunderstand or misinterpret the message or miss important pieces of data. When receiving feedback, failure to devote full attention and truly seek to understand is one of the greatest errors a person can make.

Taking Feedback at Face Value and Not Asking Questions

As we discussed previously, the feedback recipient is not simply a victim or passive receiver of feedback, although many people feel that way. The feedback recipient has control over their ability to create time and space to absorb and think about the feedback. They also have voice and autonomy to ask questions and engage in the conversation. While they cannot control the feedback provider's delivery, quality, clarity, or preparation, they *can* control what they do next. How do they react to the feedback? Do they ask questions to clarify any points that they find confusing? Do they manage their experience by saying, "I need some time to process this—let me reconnect with you later today"? One of the greatest pitfalls feedback recipients make is accepting feedback at face value, exactly as it is delivered, without asking any clarifying questions or engaging in dialogue. As we established, there are many opportunities for a feedback provider to do a poor job of delivering feedback: the feedback provider's own attitudes and beliefs about feedback, their relationship with and feelings about the recipient, how they structure the message and what they focus on in their feedback, their own level of skill and comfort giving feedback, the medium they choose to deliver it, and so on. People aren't perfect, and feedback providers are going to make mistakes. They might accidentally focus on the person instead of behavior. They may make a generalization or fail to provide evidence-based and specific feedback. Even if a feedback provider prepares in advance and plans exactly what they want to say according to feedback best practices, they are likely to unintentionally leave out some detail or piece of information that will be helpful to the recipient.

As you can see, it's likely that a feedback recipient would not get perfect information from the initial delivery. And yet, many people receive feedback "as-is" without asking questions to draw out more information or clarify anything that is unclear or confusing. When feedback recipients don't ask curious or clarifying questions about the feedback they receive, they leave the conversation with holes in their understanding regarding what they did, where or when, why it matters, and what a better performance looks like. Asking questions shows a desire to understand the feedback and figure out what can be done differently going forward to learn, grow, and perform at a higher level. Questions also help surface assumptions and biases between the two parties to ensure both are on the same page. For example, let's say your friend cooked you a lovely dinner. At the end of the meal, you show your appreciation by saying, "That was great and really fun. Thank you for making me dinner!" That sounds like normal feedback for this situation. The friend who made dinner could just accept that feedback as-is and go about their night, or they could pause to learn more and say, "What did you like most about it?" In response, you, who ate the dinner, might say,

> I really enjoyed hanging out in the kitchen with you and drinking wine and listening to music while you cooked. It's so rare to just hang out like that anymore. I am really going to treasure tonight. It made me feel special and connected to you.

If your friend assumed that you were complimenting their cooking, won't they be surprised by this more detailed feedback that focused entirely on the experience and not at all on the food! Notice what just happened: Because of one simple, seven-word question ("What did you like most about it?"), you and your friend had a meaningful moment of connection that is likely to stick with both of you, build your relationship, and potentially influence your future behavior. In the initial, very brief feedback exchange, you both made assumptions about what the other was thinking. Your friend was thinking mostly about the food, and you were thinking about the experience. This is a light and fluffy example, but the same concept applies to big deal, serious feedback. By failing to ask simple, open-ended questions to learn more, feedback recipients diminish their own learning, are much more likely to leave the conversation with assumptions or misunderstanding, and risk missing the opportunity to create a meaningful dialogue.

Expecting to Process Feedback Instantaneously

Sometimes, what gets in the way of asking questions is a failure to see that processing feedback takes time. People often expect

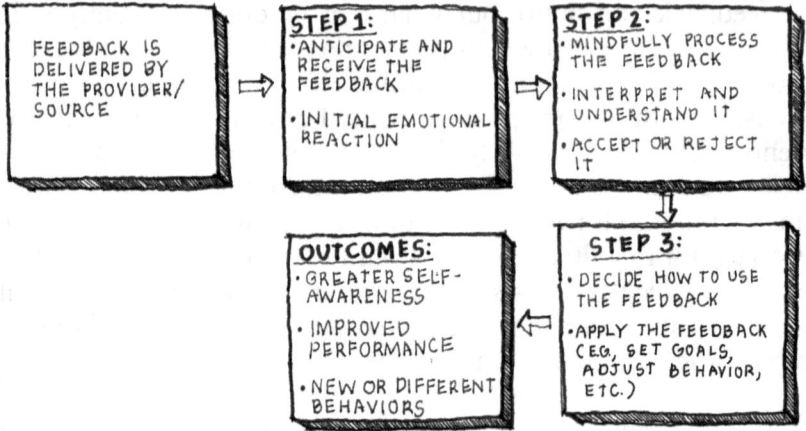

Figure 2.4 Accepting and deciding to use feedback is a multi-step process.
Adapted from London and Smither (2002).[3]

that they will be able to hear, receive, make sense of, and have a clever response to feedback, all in a matter of moments, but that is simply not how our brains work. The end-to-end act of receiving feedback consists of many steps, yet most people expect to do it all instantaneously. In their foundational work that introduced the concepts of feedback orientation and feedback culture, researchers Manuel London and James Smither (2002) outlined three stages for receiving feedback: Stage 1, which includes anticipation, receiving feedback, and initial emotional reactions; Stage 2, which focuses on processing the feedback mindfully by interpreting it, understanding the meaning and value, and accepting or rejecting the feedback; and Stage 3, which moves on to using the feedback to set goals and track progress. You can see this process in Figure 2.4.

How each stage unfolds is impacted by the feedback culture and the recipient's feedback orientation, among other individual differences. Expanding on their work, I've broken the process of receiving feedback into seven discrete steps, which could take minutes, hours, days, or weeks to unfold:

1. Hear or read the feedback
2. Have an initial emotional reaction

3. Process the feedback as rational thought catches up and emotions cool off
4. Decide whether or not to accept the feedback
5. Determine if anything is unclear or if you need more information
6. Decide what to do next
7. Do something with the feedback

Think about the last time someone gave you feedback. How much time did you allow for steps 1–5 to unfold? Feedback recipients do themselves and the feedback provider a disservice when they expect all five of these steps (and sometimes even step 6) to unfold in the moment. Really thinking about and processing feedback takes time. When feedback recipients don't recognize what they are thinking, feeling, and experiencing, or when they don't ask for what they need, they not only leave value on the table, but they also fail to assert themselves as an active participant in the conversation. It's okay to say something like "Thank you for sharing this with me. I need a little time to process the feedback and reflect. Would you be open to a follow-up conversation later this week to talk more about it?" And yet, too often, feedback recipients feel an unspoken pressure or expectation to have a great response in the moment for how they will solve the problem right away.

Remember that the whole point of the feedback exchange is to use data about the past to inform the future. Once a feedback recipient has gone through steps 1–5, a whole other world of challenges emerges where they must decide what to do with the feedback. The actual feedback exchange is full of opportunities to make stumbles and errors, and it's only the beginning! Translating feedback into action is challenging. Feedback recipients who don't really understand the issue or what they need to do about it will have a very difficult time turning feedback into action. Not knowing how to set effective goals or take small steps to start advancing on those goals will also leave feedback recipients floundering as they embark on the challenging journey of behavior change. In Chapter 5, we will focus entirely on using feedback—that is, making the pivot from receiving and making sense of feedback to setting goals, taking action, and embracing mindset and behavior change.

Box 2.1 shows a recap of what can get in the way of effective feedback exchanges.

Box 2.1 Summary of What Gets in the Way

Feedback source	The message	Context	Recipient
• The relationship between the feedback provider and the recipient • The feedback provider's attitudes and intentions • The provider's level of feedback skill	• Inappropriate feedback type (process vs. outcome) • Focused on the person rather than behavior • Not evidence-based and specific • Not clear and direct	• Waiting too long to provide feedback • Providing feedback in public • Choosing an ineffective medium	• Not managing their emotions or mindset • A weak feedback orientation • Not listening • Taking feedback at face value and not asking questions • Expecting to process the feedback instantaneously

Wrapping Up

In this chapter, we examined what can go wrong with each element in our four-element model of the feedback exchange: the source or provider of the feedback, the actual feedback message, the context in which feedback is provided, and the recipient. Now that we have defined the multifaceted problem of what gets in the way, in the remaining chapters, we'll dig into solutions: how to give, ask for and receive, and use feedback in a way that maximizes its value. Focusing only on what can go wrong feels a little bleak; let's restore hope in what's possible by exploring research-based tools and best practices that can lead to feedback exchanges that are thoughtful, effective, and strengthen relationships; drive higher performance; and support growth and development.

Try It

Notice if you are giving behavior- or person-focused feedback. If you find that you tend to give feedback to people on their personality, abilities, or character, practice reframing that feedback to focus on observable behavior. If your feedback usually includes "you *are* X," try reframing it to "you *do/did* X."

Pro Tip

Choose a mindset or think of a mental hack that helps you do hard things, like giving feedback that feels uncomfortable. Gina Thoebes, PhD, Vice President of Organizational Performance at the Arizona Cardinals Football Club, has a great example of how she prepares herself to give negative feedback. Gina says:

> It is totally normal to feel anxious about providing negative feedback. Even with all my experience and knowledge of feedback best practices, I still get a tense, yucky feeling when I have to provide someone with negative feedback. I've learned that I can't make that feeling go away, as it is part of me being a human who cares deeply for others. Instead, I intentionally choose a mindset of courage and tell myself to "step through the yuck," and deliver the feedback that my people need to be successful.

Notes

1 If you are looking for another book to read, I highly recommend "Mindset" by Carol Dweck, originally published in 2006, and most recently updated in 2017.
2 In Chapter 3, we'll talk about how to address both positive and negative feedback in the same conversation without turning it into the dreaded feedback sandwich.
3 Permission to include adapted figure obtained from Elsevier.

Give It **3**

In this chapter, we will

- Explore three steps for creating productive feedback exchanges as a feedback provider.
- Highlight several evidence-based approaches you can use to give higher-quality feedback and feel more confident and comfortable providing it.
- Take a realistic look at choices you get to make as the feedback provider, illustrated through a variety of examples.

Feedback presents a conundrum: it is, by definition, backward looking, yet we give it in an attempt to influence future behaviors and outcomes. Unless someone has a time machine, there's nothing they can do to change their past behavior. This is one reason why feedback can elicit feelings of frustration or anger. No one likes to feel like they are being judged and evaluated for something that already happened, that they can no longer influence. That's why the best feedback simply holds up a mirror, providing data about something that happened in the past, in order to help the recipient make decisions about their future behaviors. In Chapter 2, we explored the many ways that feedback exchanges can go wrong, many of which are in the control of the feedback provider. We saw that the feedback provider's intentions, mindsets, skills, and relationship with the recipient impact the exchange. The way the

DOI: 10.4324/9781003486510-3

provider constructs the actual message (feedback type and sign; focusing on person vs. behavior; how clear, specific, and evidence-based the content is) and when, where, and how they deliver it (context, timeliness, public vs. private setting, medium) have a significant impact on how the feedback is received. In this chapter, we'll look at solutions to the many problems we outlined for the feedback provider in Chapter 2. By the end of this chapter, you'll have a set of evidence-based best practices you can use immediately to be better at giving feedback.

The ability to give high-quality feedback starts before the conversation. Being a great feedback provider requires perception, or the ability to notice, as well as the ability to communicate the feedback effectively. It also requires the right mindset, which might include caring about the other person, having courage, or a desire to empower others to grow and improve by providing them with useful data. In my work over the past two decades, I have found that feedback providers often hold back from sharing feedback because of feelings of fear or anxiety about how the other person will respond or how the conversation will unfold, or self-doubt that makes them question whether or not they know what they are talking about. As organizational psychologist and author Adam Grant explained in a 2021 online post, these feelings can rob others of useful data:

> Withholding feedback is choosing comfort over growth. Staying silent deprives people of the opportunity to learn. If you're worried about hurting their feelings, it's a sign that you haven't earned their trust. In healthy relationships, honesty is an expression of care.

Even I sometimes find my own discomfort getting in the way of providing feedback. This makes me feel like a hypocrite, given my professional enthusiasm about feedback, but it's also an important reminder that providing feedback, especially to people we care about, can be intimidating. We don't want to hurt their feelings, we don't want to seem critical or controlling, we may fear how they react, we may fear how they will judge us in return, and we don't want to be wrong.

Three Steps for Effective Feedback Delivery

My goal for this chapter is to help you feel more confident and prepared to give feedback that will help others and build your relationships. We will start with three steps for effective delivery: (1) clarifying your intention; (2) planning what you will say and how, where, and when you will say it; and (3) preparing yourself to be present and give the other person space to process what you have shared. These three steps involve the three elements of our Four-Element Feedback Model that are in the hands of the provider: the source, message, and context. You'll learn actionable tools and techniques that you can use for crafting and delivering high-quality feedback, as well as effective ways to talk about "what's next" in a feedback conversation—such as how to have a dialogue, set expectations, and be a thought partner. We'll also explore some reasons or situations where you may intentionally choose NOT to share feedback. Finally, we'll take a closer look at the interplay between relationships and feedback conversations and see several examples of giving feedback in different work and life scenarios. As you read through the strategies in this chapter, keep in mind the various pitfalls that we covered in Chapter 2. In the next chapter, we'll dig into strategies to overcome the pitfalls that can trip up the feedback recipient.

Start With Your Intention

Anytime you are preparing to share feedback with someone, first ask yourself: *Why am I giving this feedback?* Is your intention to be right? To make the other person feel small or foolish? To exert your power and dominance? Or is your intention to share useful data, to help this person see a blind spot, to do something better next time, to learn and grow, to achieve their goals, or have higher performance? The true value of feedback is in providing others with useful data on their behaviors in order to help them learn, adjust their behavior, or have greater self-awareness. From a control theory perspective, feedback is useful because it helps others assess their current state with respect to their goals or desired state. Having a clear intention will help you decide what to say and how to say it. Having a "why" for sharing your feedback—a clear objective or sense of purpose—will make the interaction feel more constructive, productive, and authentic. Your intention could be something like

- My friend Elijah frequently talks over or interrupts people. He did it to me this morning when we met for coffee. *I want to share that feedback with him because it might help him improve his interactions in the future with me and others, and because I care about him.*
- The volunteer leader of the non-profit I work with sends really clear and interesting weekly updates. It helps me and other volunteers know what's coming up, about opportunities to be involved, and the impact of our work. *I want to tell her how clear and helpful her weekly emails are, so she knows we really appreciate her work, that her emails help us be better volunteers, and because I want her to keep sending them.*
- This is my favorite restaurant and during my last two visits, something was incorrect with my order. *I want to let them know so they can address the issue and continue to be a successful business.*
- Oliver keeps doing this task wrong and no one is telling him. Other colleagues just fix it later and he is unaware. *I want to give him feedback that he is not doing the task correctly so he can learn how to do it correctly going forward, so we won't have to do rework in the future, and so he doesn't look incompetent in front of our peers.*

You may notice in the examples above that the intention was always about helping or supporting the other person, not about trying to feel powerful or superior, or making the other person feel bad or small. Remember, the reason we give feedback is to influence future behavior. We want to hold up the mirror so others can be more self-aware and empowered to use the valuable data that we share with them about their behaviors. Taking a few minutes to check in with yourself about why you are giving this feedback and what you hope to achieve with it will help you get your head in the right place, have clear purpose for your feedback, and feel more confident in the value of giving the feedback. If your intention is anything *other* than to help or share data, ask yourself why you are considering giving the feedback, what you are hoping to accomplish, and if sharing the feedback is in the other person's best interest. If you were on the receiving side, would you want this feedback?

Plan What, How, Where, and When

Once you have set your intention, map out what exactly you want to say (the message) and how, where, and when you want to deliver it (the context; see Figure 3.1). I'm often amazed when I encounter managers and team leaders in organizations who don't take a few minutes to collect their thoughts before providing feedback to their teams or colleagues. You will always deliver feedback that is higher quality, clearer, and easier for the receiver to use when you invest a few minutes into thinking it through in advance. Particularly with challenging or uncomfortable feedback, a few minutes spent planning, writing down, or saying aloud what you want to get across will ensure that you're saying what you really intend to say and surfacing anything that could be misconstrued or isn't clear. It will also help you feel more comfortable giving the feedback.

What

The crux of the feedback exchange is the actual message that you share. What do you want to say? What is important about the observation? Start by jotting down whatever thoughts and observations first come to mind, but don't stop there. If you are like most humans, your initial thoughts will be general, maybe a little vague or focused on the person. If that's where you start

WHAT	HOW, WHERE, AND WHEN
FOCUSED ON BEHAVIOR	VIA THE APPROPRIATE MEDIUM
EVIDENCE-BASED	TIMELY
SPECIFIC	IN PRIVATE

Figure 3.1 Plan what, how, where, and when.

when formulating your thoughts or talking points, that's okay . . . the key is to push yourself to ensure that your feedback is ultimately *focused on behavior* (never the person), *evidence-based*, and *specific*. For example, I might start formulating my thoughts with my overall impression that "Elijah is rude. He always interrupts people." Now, let's dig in on that headline and turn it into high-quality feedback that won't make our conversation with Elijah feel like a debate. Instead, I might say, "Elijah, I have noticed a pattern where you interrupt or talk over people. This morning when we met for coffee you interrupted me three times." What do you notice is different about that latter version? Although I start with a pattern, I am able to provide a specific, behavioral, evidence-based example with "This morning when we met for coffee you interrupted me three times." Let's break down why these three characteristics of feedback are so important.

Focused on Behavior

Recall from Chapter 2 that giving someone feedback about who they are as a person is a fast lane to an unhelpful conversation. Feedback that focuses on behaviors, rather than the person, is much easier for the receiver to digest and act on. Remember that the whole point of giving feedback is to help people consider changes to their future behavior. Feedback Intervention Theory (Kluger & DeNisi, 1996) suggests that feedback focused on the person is more likely to direct attention inward to the self and distract from learning about performance on the task or behavior. For example, negative feedback focused on you as a person shifts your attention inward to *you* (to feelings of self-consciousness, tending to your emotions, defending yourself, etc.) as opposed to keeping the focus on your behavior, the impact or why it matters, and what you can learn from the feedback.

Unsurprisingly, research has shown that person-focused feedback can diminish the quality and impact of a feedback exchange. One study found that individuals who received person-focused feedback (focused on their intelligence or on labeling them as a hard worker) were less likely to enjoy the task they were working on, had lower perceptions of their own success, and were more likely to attribute their failures to lack of intelligence, compared to individuals who received feedback on their efforts (behavior) (Reavis et al., 2018). Another study found that providing behavior-focused feedback on someone's racist behaviors was more likely to result in a constructive conversation than person-focused feedback that labeled them as a racist (Wessel et al., 2023). These researchers found that feedback focused on racist behaviors was more likely to lead to prosocial behavior, such as developing plans for self-improvement. In contrast, the person-focused feedback was more likely to lead to reactions like hostility, withdrawal, and avoidance.

When you are preparing to give feedback, if you find yourself focusing first on the person, push yourself to the next step: What exactly are they doing or not doing? What is their behavior that you want to share feedback on? So you can see what this looks like, Figure 3.2 contrasts examples of person-focused feedback you might be tempted to give with those examples reframed to focus on behavior.

Notice that in the two person-focused examples, the feedback says, "You *are* [unreliable/a rockstar]." The *are* portion of the feedback is labeling the person, whereas the revised behavior-focused feedback targets specific behaviors or actions, such as not calling, arriving late, speaking succinctly and answering questions, or promptly resolving a customer complaint—all things that the

PERSON-FOCUSED	REFRAMED TO FOCUS ON BEHAVIOR
YOU'RE UNRELIABLE	THE LAST TWO TIMES YOU SAID YOU WOULD CALL ME YOU DID NOT CALL ME. YOU WERE SUPPOSED TO BE HERE AT 5 PM TO BABYSIT. YOU ARRIVED HERE AT 6:15 PM AND DID NOT CALL OR TEXT TO LET ME KNOW YOU WERE RUNNING LATE.
YOU ARE A ROCKSTAR!	IN YOUR PRESENTATION TODAY YOU HIT ALL THREE KEY POINTS VERY CLEARLY. YOU SPOKE SUCCINCTLY AND THOROUGHLY ANSWERED EVERYONE'S QUESTIONS. YOU RESOLVED THAT CUSTOMER COMPLAINT PROMPTLY AND THEY LEFT FEELING SATISFIED WITH THE OUTCOME.

Figure 3.2 Contrasting person-focused versus behavior-focused feedback.

person *did*. Imagine yourself on the receiving end of both types of feedback. What feels different about hearing "You are unreliable" or "You are a rockstar" compared to the behavior-focused examples? If you are like many people, you would likely be motivated to defend yourself after being called unreliable. Rather than learning about what you did or didn't do and the impact, as you would from behavioral feedback, you might feel hijacked by the label and engage in debate with the feedback provider. Similarly, you might feel a few moments of positive emotion after being called a rockstar but probably won't learn much from that platitude. I like to call feedback like this "empty calorie" feedback, as explained in Box 3.1.

Box 3.1 Empty Calorie Feedback

Sharing high-level platitudes is like only eating candy. It might taste good for a moment, but contains little substance or value. Empty calorie feedback sounds like:

"You're amazing!"
"You are brilliant!"
"You're such a rockstar"

Heard these before? They probably felt good for a moment but did little (or nothing) to help you understand exactly what it was you did well or why it matters.

When providing positive feedback, follow the same best practices as you would for negative feedback. Focus on observable behaviors with evidence and be specific. Next time you catch yourself giving that empty calorie feedback, catch yourself in the act, and follow it with something substantive to help the other person understand what exactly they did that leads you to the conclusion they are amazing, brilliant, a rockstar, or some other ego-boosting but data-poor label.

If the goal of giving feedback is to help the receiver understand the impact of their actions or behaviors or to influence future behavior, then labeling them with person-focused feedback (e.g., "you are amazing/annoying/disruptive, etc.") is unlikely to move the needle. Providing clear feedback that focuses on what they did or did not do is more likely to help them gain self-awareness and motivate them to keep doing or do more of a good behavior, or prompt them to adjust their behavior to something more effective in the future.

Evidence-Based

When focusing our feedback on behaviors, we want to be sure to be as evidence-based as possible, which means focusing on facts—concrete events or observations—and holding up a mirror to the recipient. Evidence-based feedback requires focusing only on things you can see with your eyes (or hear, taste, or smell) and avoiding assumptions about *why* someone did what they did, their motivations, what they were thinking, or what they intended. Providing strictly evidence-based feedback eliminates the risk of making assumptions or letting personal biases or preferences influence what we share. As a result, the feedback sometimes sounds a little dry . . . and that's okay!

Let's use one of our previous examples of behavior-focused feedback to illustrate: "You were supposed to be here at 5 pm to babysit. You arrived here at 6:15 pm and did not call or text to let me know you were running late." That is fact-based and observable. If we go the next step to add something like "I know you don't really care about my plans or my schedule," or ". . . because you don't think this job is important," or ". . . because you communicate like a Gen Z," we cease to be evidence-based, and the conversation takes a turn in the wrong direction. Do we have any evidence to support any of those claims? Unless you have had a prior conversation where the person specifically revealed their beliefs or intentions to you, or you can see inside their mind, you probably don't know that any of these are true. They are merely your assumptions. And by adding your assumptions to your feedback, you immediately shift the conversation from one that is productive, constructive, and focused on the issue at hand, to one where the other person will want to debate and defend themselves. Often, feedback providers over-function by trying to diagnose or solve what they perceive as wrong with the other person. But your job as a feedback provider is simply to share data. You don't need to fix the other person or solve their challenge for them, and in fact, they will be more motivated if they decide for themselves what they want to do with the feedback and how to resolve the matter (more on that later). I frequently hear feedback providers say something akin to "they did XYZ because they think/feel ABC." As much as you think you know what someone was thinking or why they did something, you probably do not. Even if you could read their minds, most people don't like to be told what they think or why they did something. Making assumptions about their motivations and intentions will only derail your feedback conversations.

Technology can be superior to humans when it comes to giving truly evidence-based feedback. Technology does not make assumptions about *why* someone did something; it simply provides data on what the person did or did not do. It enables real-time feedback that is specific, objective, and devoid of emotion. And research has shown that people are open to feedback that comes directly from technology. Bernstein and Li (2017) found that employees believe that evidence-based tech-generated performance data is more transparent than feedback derived from another person's subjective observations. These researchers found that when employees are provided with system-generated feedback that tells them how they are tracking against goals or standards, they engage in fewer non-productive activities and have higher subsequent performance. These gains were even higher for employees who felt unsupported by their managers. The ability to get straightforward, task-focused performance feedback without engaging with their manager or peers empowered these employees to make better use of their time and increase their productivity.

One study of university students found that feedback generated directly from technology (specifically, large language models, or LLMs) led students to revise their work and have better output, feel motivated to use the feedback to improve their work, and feel positive emotions in response to the feedback they received (Meyer et al., 2024). Another study found that AI-generated negative feedback led to higher motivation to learn, improved performance, and less rumination compared to similar feedback provided by a human; these findings were even more pronounced for participants who had a strong "fear of losing face," or concern about how others would perceive them based on the negative feedback (Pei et al., 2024). Feedback from human-like avatars powered by artificial intelligence is also effective for providing evidence-based feedback without judgment. A study of job applicants found that avatar-provided feedback on job interview performance led participants to have lower anxiety, communicate more effectively (such as better word choice and vocal pitch), and have higher performance on a second interview after receiving the feedback (Hosseini et al., 2024)

A friend recently told me about a wellness app on her phone that is helping her stay motivated and make lasting changes. She established goals for weight loss, exercise, and diet and uses the app to track her progress toward those goals:

> I input what I eat and my exercise and the app gives me feedback on how I'm doing. It gives me positive feedback every few weeks about my successes and shows me how I'm tracking against my goals. It also provides short-term reinforcement. If I eat three vegetables in one day I get a dancing broccoli icon, thumbs up for drinking enough water, and also immediate feedback on foods I'm eating that are not very healthy. This feedback has helped me learn a lot about the nutritional value of the foods I'm eating. I've always had trouble sticking to a diet, but this one is fun and helps me stay motivated. I can track how I'm doing against my goals and get immediate reinforcement. This app has helped me build new habits and truly change my lifestyle.

Notice she doesn't take the app's feedback personally or feel like she is being judged by the app. The same reaction is possible when humans deliver feedback. Over the years, I have come to believe that the keys to providing high-quality feedback are the abilities to *notice* and to *communicate* what you have noticed. Noticing starts with attention; it's all about picking up on observations about others' behaviors and the impact of those behaviors (noticing can also pertain to picking up on observations about yourself, the world around you, etc., but for our purposes we're focused on others' behavior). A hallmark of noticing is that it is free from judgment and interpretation; it's simply about making objective observations and collecting data. For example, when I look around my office, I can *notice* that there are three coffee mugs and a stack of papers on my desk. That is objective and evidence-based

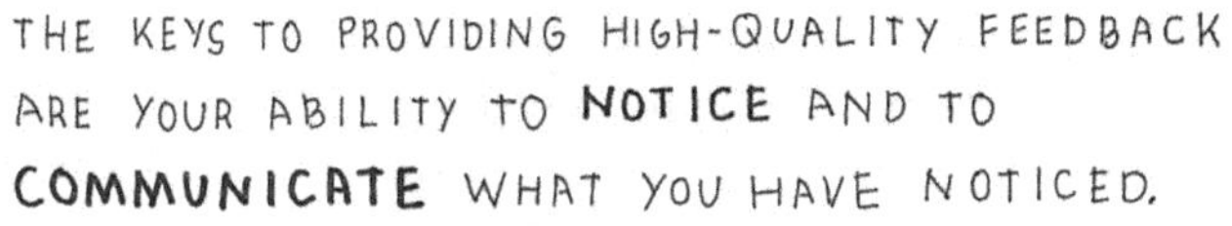

THE KEYS TO PROVIDING HIGH-QUALITY FEEDBACK
ARE YOUR ABILITY TO **NOTICE** AND TO
COMMUNICATE WHAT YOU HAVE NOTICED.

Figure 3.3 Giving high-quality feedback starts before the conversation.

data. A judgment or interpretation would sound more like "my desk is messy." See the difference? Similarly, my friend's app noticed when she ate vegetables or when she ate junk food, and it communicated that data back to her; it didn't admonish her to eat better. The same is true when we notice others' behavior and communicate our observations to them through feedback. Evidence-based feedback would sound like "You consumed seven plastic water bottles today and put them all in the trash rather than recycling them." Instead, if we said, "You are wasteful and don't care about the environment," we are judging and interpreting their behavior (and also focusing on the person!).

Remember that our mission as a feedback provider is to share objective data and hold up the mirror. And the more specific our feedback is, the easier it will be for the other person to understand it and do something with it.

Specific

I'm going to sound like a broken record here but remember the primary reason we give feedback is to inform future behavior. And the more specific feedback is, the easier it is to translate into future behaviors. Behavior change is hard, and the more general or abstract feedback is, the harder it is to figure out what specifically was good or bad about one's behavior and what to do differently in the future. Kluger and DeNisi's (1996) Feedback Intervention Theory (FIT) points out the importance of *levels of abstraction* for feedback to translate to meaningful behavior change. A high level of abstraction means that something is general, macro, or overarching. A low level of abstraction means something is specific. Humans adjust their behavior at low levels of abstraction. High-level, general feedback (e.g., a high level of abstraction) is more challenging to translate into behavior change than specific feedback (e.g., a low level of abstraction). Recall the example from Chapter 1 where we told a leader that they "need to develop their executive presence." Feedback like this gets thrown around all the time in organizations. I have heard it myself for dozens of leaders I have worked with in executive coaching engagements. The problem with this well-intended but vague feedback is that it doesn't tell the leader anything specific about their behavior; it is an example of a high level of abstraction. If, instead, the feedback provider pushed themselves a step further to give more specific feedback (a lower level of abstraction), they would be able to highlight specific things that led to their general feedback about executive presence, such as that the leader looked at the floor rather than the audience when they were delivering a presentation yesterday, or that they stood quietly in the corner and only spoke briefly to one client during an event that morning, or that in the leadership team meeting last week, they crossed their arms, hunched over, had a furrowed brow, and looked at their phone the whole time. All of these examples highlight very specific actions that the leader took (or didn't take) and could easily be generalized into "executive presence." The specific pieces of feedback allow the leader to understand what they did (or didn't do) and know what actions or behaviors they need to target if they want to do something different next time.

I also want to reiterate that telling a leader they need to "develop their executive presence" isn't actually feedback, it's advice. Recall from Chapter 1 that adults' brains are not actively engaged when receiving advice (Engelmann et al., 2009); we passively shift out of thinking and problem solving and have less of a sense of ownership for the solution. Providing specific feedback also means leaving out extreme language, like "always" or "never." Sweeping generalizations about a person—such as "you always get home late from work" or "you never listen to me when I am talking to you"—are more likely to result in the recipient getting defensive. Once again, the real value of the feedback is lost, and the conversation devolves into a debate about what this person actually does or doesn't do.

One of my favorite tools for ensuring that feedback is specific (and also behavior-focused and evidence-based) is the Situation-Behavior-Impact model (SBI; Weitzel, 2000). I learned about this model years ago during a workshop with the Center for Creative Leadership and have been using it myself ever since. The SBI model helps you plan out and articulate what you want to say, increasing the likelihood that your feedback will be clear, specific, and direct. Following the three-part SBI model, your feedback message will include the *situation* (S) where the behavior occurred, the specific *behavior* (B), and the *impact* (I)—why it matters. For example, let's say you saw pictures on social media of several of your friends together on a trip. Your feelings were really hurt that you weren't included in the trip. Using the SBI model, you could say to one or all of the friends: "Yesterday, I saw pictures on Instagram of the three of you in Costa Rica (situation). You did not include me in this trip (behavior), and my feelings were really hurt (impact)." Notice this feedback does not make any inferences about why your friends didn't include you or make any judgments about them. This feedback simply, but specifically, articulates what they did, in what situation, and why it matters to you. You can even try it with kids: "Jonah, at the soccer game today you left the snacks open on the ground and the containers got filled with ants. As a result, none of your teammates were able to have a snack at the end of the game." This example actually has a double impact: because Jonah left the snacks open (behavior), the snacks filled with ants (impact) and as a result of that, no one was able to eat snacks (a secondary impact).

Using the SBI model and remaining evidence-based will help you avoid making assumptions about *why* the other person behaved the way they did.[1] You will undoubtedly have hypotheses about their behavior but remember that you simply cannot see into their minds. Even if you are *right* in your assumptions about the other person, they are more likely to get defensive or deny your feedback if there is not objective evidence to support your points.

How, Where, and When

Once you have figured out *what* you want to say (and ensured your feedback is behavior-focused, evidence-based, and specific), your next decision is about context: how, where, and when you will share the feedback. *How* pertains to the medium that you select, such as having an in-person, face-to-face conversation, a phone call or video call; sharing written feedback in an email or document; or using tools like texting or instant message. *Where* and *when* you provide your feedback pertains to timing and the setting, such as being in private or publicly sharing feedback in front of other people. You'll recall from Chapter 2 that a wide array of pitfalls stem from poor choices about how and when to deliver feedback. Let's focus now on choices that will increase the likelihood that your feedback exchange goes well.

How

As a feedback provider, you have many options for how to provide feedback. You can give feedback face to face, which includes both in person and video calls. You can give feedback verbally over the phone, in writing via email or document (such as a written narrative or comments on a Word document), or via text or instant message. You can even provide feedback on public platforms, such as Google Reviews, Yelp, or thousands of other websites and applications. Each method has advantages and disadvantages. Feedback delivered face to face—whether in person or via video—enables both the feedback provider and the recipient to see one another's facial expressions and body language, which are important when the feedback may evoke strong emotions. On the other hand, face-to-face feedback is also the most likely to be inflated—that is, negative feedback tends to be more lenient and less direct compared to written feedback (Waung & Highhouse, 1997), likely because people are uncomfortable giving direct feedback face to face. Research has shown that verbal feedback (such as meeting in person or over the phone) is the most commonly used method of delivering feedback but is actually most effective when paired with something in writing or a visual that the recipient can refer to (Alvero et al., 2001; Au & Chan, 2013). People see feedback as fairer when it is shared on a phone call rather than text message, and email is also a preferred channel, particularly when the recipient considers the provider to be highly credible (Au & Chan, 2013; Baker et al., 2025; Westerman et al., 2015). One advantage of email-based feedback is that it can be immediate, yet the recipient has some discretion and control over when and where they choose to read it and take action. Feedback sent via text- or instant message, on the other hand, conveys an immediacy and can be more intrusive than email-based feedback, and is therefore best suited to quick, just-in-time or in-the-moment feedback about relatively inconsequential topics.

For example, if I were at a party and had a big piece of parsley on my front tooth, I would most prefer my friend at the party tell me face to face when we get a private moment. If that wasn't possible, a quick, discreet text might let me take quick action if I have my phone or an Apple watch on me. In another situation, however, when a client let me know that we did not succeed in securing a new piece of work with them, I really appreciated a phone call to share the news and some detailed feedback about why. A text would have felt flippant and dismissive; an email would have felt impersonal. A face-to-face conversation wasn't realistic with geographic constraints. The same goes for positive feedback. When sharing very exciting positive news or praise, consider which medium will best convey the message. Letting someone know that they got promoted via text message may feel anticlimactic. A face-to-face discussion could make the news seem all the more exciting and celebratory (via video if in-person is not realistic). On the other hand, if you work on a remote team and want to share positive feedback with a team member about a virtual presentation they just delivered, an instant message or email will provide the timely reinforcement that could get lost if you waited to have a face-to-face conversation.

Where and When

Timing can make or break the success of a feedback exchange. In general, the sooner feedback is provided after the focal "event," the better. The longer you wait, the more the memory of the event fades in both your mind and the mind of the feedback recipient. The sooner feedback is delivered the more likely people are to pay attention to it and also to act on it (van der Kleij et al., 2012). Sharing feedback soon after the event also shows that you care. Waiting days or weeks to share feedback suggests to the recipient that this isn't a priority for you. Several studies have shown that the longer someone has to wait for feedback, the less they engage with it and the less relevant it feels to them (Poulos & Mahony, 2008; Winstone et al., 2017). The opportunity for course correcting or acting on feedback may have passed, too, when feedback is delayed.

You'll recall from Chapter 2 that one caveat to giving feedback as soon as possible is waiting until you are in the right setting. Most people are very uncomfortable receiving feedback in a public setting, in front of others. Delay your feedback delivery until you can be in a private setting, particularly when the feedback is negative or might make the recipient feel embarrassed. Positive feedback and praise can be tricky—some people love to be praised in front of their peers or colleagues, whereas others feel embarrassed. When in doubt, err on the side of privacy. Not only can public praise make the recipient uncomfortable, but it can also make the people observing the conversation uncomfortable (Chan & Sengupta, 2013). Ultimately, the better you know the person you are providing feedback to, the better able you will be to make smart choices about how, where, and when to provide feedback. You'll also recall that another reason to wait to share your feedback is if either you or the recipient is experiencing strong emotions (positive or negative) and will be better able to engage in the conversation when you wait for those emotions to cool off.

In Chapter 2, we mentioned the dreaded feedback sandwich, where you "sandwich" a piece of negative feedback between two pieces of positive feedback in an effort to make the conversation easier. Of course, we know now that the feedback sandwich usually results in people feeling confused or unclear about what the issue is or learning to anticipate negative feedback after they receive positive feedback. In short, avoid the feedback sandwich. But is it okay to share both positive and negative feedback in the same conversation? This question comes up a lot in workshops, particularly when managers are preparing to have a review conversation, and my answer is yes, you can share both positive and negative feedback in the same conversation and still avoid the feedback sandwich. There is a difference between giving a feedback sandwich and signaling in a conversation that you are going to share both positive and negative feedback. If you find yourself in this position, be clear with the recipient about your intentions for the conversation, such as "Eileen, I want to share with you two examples of ways you have had positive impact on this team, and one observation about a behavior that is getting in the way of you communicating clearly with customers." In the conversation, share the detailed (behavioral, evidence-based, specific) feedback about the two positive observations. Then pause to see what questions or thoughts Eileen has before moving on to the negative piece of feedback, signaling to Eileen that you are shifting to your other observations. Share your negative feedback (again ensuring your feedback is behavioral, evidence-based, and specific!), then pause again to create space for Eileen to respond. This leads us to our final step for high-quality feedback delivery: being present and giving space.

Be Present and Give Space

Once you have figured out what you want to say, and how, where, and when you will deliver your feedback, the third step is to be mentally present and attentive and give the other person space to process and respond. You might find that this step requires the most self-management. At its core, feedback is a very human interaction. As a feedback provider, you have doubts, insecurities, fears, and assumptions that make giving feedback challenging. Feedback recipients have a similar set of fears, anxieties, doubt, and dread that have developed from years of unpleasant feedback exchanges. When you connect with one another as humans first, the feedback exchange is easier and can lead to meaningful changes in future behavior. As a feedback provider, you not only choose when, where, and how to deliver feedback, but you also have control over the "human conditions" of the feedback exchange. One of the greatest gifts you can give to the other person is your full attention, meaning that you are physically, mentally, and emotionally present *in* the conversation and not distracted. Being fully mindful and present will not only enable you to be a better listener and ensure the other person feels respected and heard, but it will also help you overcome your own anxieties and self-doubts about the conversation. Mindfulness plays an important role in managing anxiety and reducing self-consciousness (Brown & Ryan, 2003), freeing up your attention to focus on the present situation, not your fears and doubts.

Set yourself up for success by eliminating distractions that will get in the way of you being fully present and attentive. If possible, select a location where you can truly focus on the conversation— not in a busy common area or a "fishbowl" office where everyone who walks by catches your eye. Most of all, set your technology aside! Leave your phone in your bag or desk or set it to "do not disturb" mode so you will not be distracted by ringing or vibrating with calls, texts, or other notifications. Research has shown that simply hearing your phone buzz—even if you don't look at the notification—distracts attention (Upshaw et al., 2022). An interruption as simple as one text alert creates cognitive overload and divided attention that undermines our ability to stay present and focused in the conversation. You'll also want to close your laptop, or, if you need to use it for the feedback exchange, hide and silence notifications and shut down any unnecessary apps that might pull your attention away from the conversation (that includes email notifications, Slack, Teams, instant messenger, etc.)

A colleague once shared a story with me about a feedback conversation she had over the phone with her manager. Her manager had shared feedback with her about things she could work on to be more effective in her role. After he shared the feedback, she responded about some of the challenges and self-doubts that were getting in her way. In the background she could hear her manager typing on his computer. He was either distracted or attempting to multitask, but that one moment in their conversation deeply eroded her trust and respect for her manager. He was going through the motions of listening (lots of "uh-huhs") but was not actually present in the conversation. If you struggle with distraction or a temptation to multitask, do whatever necessary to create the right conditions for an effective conversation—meet in person, have a video conference rather than a phone call, go to a room where you will not be distracted by technology, other people, or anything else that might pull you away from the feedback recipient.

One common pitfall for recipients that we highlighted in Chapter 2 was the problem of not really listening. But listening is also imperative for feedback providers to effectively engage in the conversation. Really listening means giving your full attention to the other person and responding in a way that makes them feel heard and understood, which is particularly important in a challenging feedback exchange. You'll also want to be sure you are truly listening to understand the other person and respond about *them*, not yourself. Self-focused listening, when we listen with ourselves in mind, is sometimes referred to as "level 1" listening. We hear what others say and respond in relation to ourselves, rather than really hearing the other person (Whitworth et al., 2009). For example, in a feedback conversation about their team meetings, Asia shares that she thinks the meetings are not effective because they lack a structured agenda. When Asia's manager responds, "You think those meetings are bad? You should see the monthly management meetings that I have to go to!" Asia does not feel heard and instead feels like her manager deflected her feedback and tried to one-up her by talking about how bad this other meeting is. This response may have been Asia's manager's attempt at empathy, connection, or humor, but ultimately the manager's response led to a missed opportunity to hear her team member and work together to improve a work process. Asia's manager listened and responded at level 1—she made the conversation about herself, rather than Asia's feedback and feelings. Another common mistake in trying to show empathy is telling people how they *should* or should not feel. In an effort to put the recipient at ease or help them feel better, it may be tempting to say "Oh, you shouldn't feel that way," but in reality, this response simply discounts or minimizes how they actually feel. Rather, lean on your curiosity and keep the other person in the spotlight with a response like "Tell me more about what makes you feel that way," or acknowledge their emotion, "Sounds like you find this situation frustrating."

Finally, give space. Recall from Chapter 2 that the process of receiving feedback requires both cognitive and emotional effort, and those two systems operate on different timelines. Emotional reactions occur much faster than our ability to rationally, cognitively process information. As a result, the recipient will need time to pause, process, and absorb the feedback you've provided. This might require a pause in the conversation and potentially some silence, which makes most people pretty uncomfortable. Silence may simply mean the other person is experiencing their immediate emotional reaction and taking time to process what you said. Don't get in their way! If you are uncomfortable with silence and tend to fill it with rambling and unnecessary talking, plan ahead to get out of your own way. Experiment with techniques to see what works for you—such as counting to 15, taking three deep breaths, singing the "Happy Birthday" song in your head (which takes about 15–20 seconds), or adopting a short phrase that you

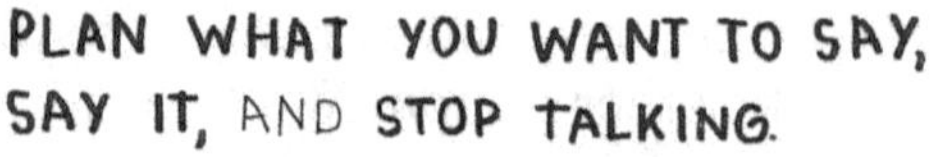

PLAN WHAT YOU WANT TO SAY,
SAY IT, AND STOP TALKING.

Figure 3.4 Set yourself up for success when you deliver feedback.

can repeat to yourself, like "stop talking, wait, give them space."
You can even use your physical body to help you, such as touching
each finger to the side of your chair a few times or tapping your
toes on the floor 20 times. The key here is to find something that
works for you to create and protect a pause that provides the
other person time to think and respond.

When you need to give feedback that makes you a bit uncomfortable, *plan what you are going to say, say it, and then stop
talking.* Don't dig yourself into a hole by rambling on. More
words are not better, and in fact, they can muddy your message
and make the recipient feel as though they are being lectured.
Remember from Chapter 2 that the process of receiving feedback
consists of many steps and one of the most important variables in
that process is time.

What Next?

One question that comes up often in workshops and discussions
about feedback is, after I deliver the feedback, then what? Great
question. As we know, feedback exchanges do not take place in
a vacuum; they occur in the context of existing relationships and
ongoing work. After you provide feedback (and allow time and
space for the other person to process), you have several options
for what happens next, including turning the conversation into a
dialogue and sharing expectations or what behaviors you want to
see in the future.

Turning the Conversation Into a Dialogue

Dialogic feedback is a particular approach to feedback that has
been researched extensively for its application in education.
Dialogic feedback emphasizes a back-and-forth, collaborative

discussion between the educator and student, as opposed to one-way feedback from the educator (Blair & McGinty, 2013; Dochy et al., 2022). This approach emphasizes several characteristics, such as active listening, open-ended questions, prompt feedback, and a focus on learning. This approach to feedback makes the student an active part of the conversation, as opposed to a passive recipient. The same is true of effective feedback outside of educational settings. The best feedback conversations are exactly that: conversations. Feedback delivered in a one-way manner—what I like to call "drop and run" feedback, where the provider drops the feedback on the other person and moves on—leaves so much opportunity on the table.

There are several ways that feedback providers can invite the recipient into the conversation and turn it into a dialogue. One of the best ways is by asking an open-ended question after sharing the feedback. Simple questions can be a way to invite the recipient to be an active participant in the conversation: "How is this landing with you?" or "What else would be helpful to know?" or "How can I best help you?" Notice that none of those questions could be answered with yes or no. Focusing on open-ended questions here is essential, because they draw out information and open up the conversation, as opposed to closing down the discussion with a mere yes-or-no response. Here, we draw a bit on coaching skills, where we know that some of the very best questions start with "what," "how," "tell me more," or "I'm curious about . . ." Some of the most effective open-ended questions are no more than five or six words and contain minimal pre-amble or post-amble. These types of questions are powerful because they give ownership for next steps or solutions to the feedback recipient.

I mentioned this before, but it's worth repeating: As feedback provider, your responsibility is to hold up the mirror and share the data with the recipient, *not* to solve their problem for them. Sure, you might share some thoughts on what "better" looks like or explain your expectations for what happens next (more on that shortly), but the recipient will be much more motivated about a solution they came up with themselves, as opposed to one that was told to them by the feedback provider. Once the feedback provider shares their feedback and asks an open-ended question to invite the recipient in, they must shift into "really listening" mode, using not only their ears but also their full attention, and seeking to understand, not to judge or to map out what they want to say next. How the provider responds to follow-up questions from the recipient is also important. Rather than feeling defensive or annoyed by follow-up questions, feedback providers will want to have a mindset of curiosity, seeking to understand or support the recipient, or seeing themselves as a thought partner, rather than getting defensive or annoyed with their questions. When recipients ask questions, it usually means they want to understand the feedback and might be trying to fill in some gaps in what they heard. Those questions might also pertain to what "better" looks like. Sometimes, in these discussions, the feedback provider may also need to share expectations or their perspective on what higher performance means.

Setting Expectations or Desired Behaviors

Think back to what you learned in Chapter 1 about control theory: feedback stems from comparing a current state with some goal or desired state. Anytime we share feedback, it is in reference to some such standard. Sometimes in a feedback conversation, you will need to make sure that you and the recipient have a shared understanding of expectations, or what behavior you want to see from them. Recall our discussion of the three-part Situation-Behavior-Impact (SBI) model (Weitzel, 2000). There is an optional fourth piece to this model, which is the Desired Behavior (now it's the SBID model). Let's revisit our example of Jonah and the snacks at the soccer game from our initial discussion of the SBI model. If we were to add a "D" (desired behavior) to that example, it might sound something like this:

> Jonah, at the soccer game today (S) you left the snacks open on the ground (B) and the containers got filled with ants (I). As a result, none of your teammates were able to have a snack at the end of the game (I). *Next time please wait until the end of the game to open the snacks, or if you open the snacks make sure you completely close the containers so ants can't get inside* (D).

In this example, you are clearly articulating to Jonah your expectation for future behavior or what "better" looks like.

Note that sharing your Desired Behavior is not the same as giving advice. You are articulating what you want or expect from the other person. Clearly setting and articulating expectations plays an important role in feedback conversations, and yet I have found that this is something that people struggle with in all manner of jobs, industries, roles, and other areas of life. Ages ago, I worked with an awesome researcher, professor, and consultant named Neta Moye who introduced me to a framework that makes setting and clarifying expectations nearly foolproof. I like to think of this framework as a "Mad Lib" for expectations: Do [what] to/for/with [whom] by [when] to [what standard] and here's [why]. By filling in the gaps—either when you are communicating an expectation or clarifying an expectation that someone else has shared with you (if you are the recipient)—you surface any assumptions or missing pieces of data. Incorporating the Mad Lib framework[2] into a feedback discussion will ensure that the provider and recipient are aligned and have a shared understanding of what needs to happen next.

Because the intent of feedback is to inform future behavior, some research has explored ways to make feedback conversations feel more forward-looking. Once again, we see the conundrum of feedback: it can be frustrating to receive because it is by definition backward looking. The recipient can't change what they did in the past, so the feedback may lead to them feeling criticized, judged, or helpless. Adding a *forward-looking lens* to the conversation can offer a chance at redemption, encouraging the recipient to use feedback on past events as data points to inform future behavior (Roberts et al., 2019). For example, putting a forward-looking lens on the feedback conversation can help to "broaden and build" (Fredrickson, 2001) the recipients' emotional reactions and (in response to negative feedback) it can encourage creative problem solving (Roberts et al., 2019). Rather than getting defensive, dwelling on negative emotions, or pushing back on the feedback, a recipient who is encouraged to think about what they will do next time the situation occurs may be more likely to accept and use the feedback.

Research on best practices for forward-looking feedback is limited, and you'll want to be careful not slip into advice-giving, but there are a few pieces of evidence that suggest the possibilities of being forward looking. Feedback providers can help encourage a forward-looking feedback conversation by articulating what "better" would look like in the future or by using open-ended questions to help the recipient think through the "next time" opportunity. Positive psychology techniques like Appreciative Inquiry and visualization can help with processing feedback and thinking through how to use it in detail (O'Malley & Gregory, 2011). Like coaching, Appreciative Inquiry engages others through thoughtful, non-judgmental questions to draw out their ideas about what could be possible in the future (Cooperrider & Srivastva, 1987). Visualization encourages the feedback recipient to get concrete and specific about what they will do in the future and (O'Malley et al., 2009; Ungerleider, 2005). Visualization, which activates the same neural networks as the actual behavior, has been shown to drive higher performance for athletes and elicit positive emotions that lead to improved performance in the workplace (Kauffman, 2006; Ungerleider, 2005). Questions as simple as "When you present on next month's investor call, what will you do differently?" and "Tell me what success on that will look and feel like" can shift feedback recipients out of an emotional downward spiral and into constructive, future-focused problem-solving mode following negative feedback. You may not have a time machine, but you can provide the next best thing by giving the feedback recipient a chance for a "do over" when the conversation is forward looking and future focused.

When Not to Give Feedback

Another question I am frequently asked is: "Are there times when I should *not* give feedback?" There are several reasons why you might intentionally choose not to share feedback with someone. If you have a low-trust relationship with that person, you might choose to hold back on sharing some of your observations. Sharing useful data, skillfully, at the right time will help you to build trust with that person, but telling them every single thing on your mind might undermine your efforts. You can always try the strategy that I like to call, "dip a toe"—that is, share one small, useful, actionable piece of feedback with that person and see what happens. If they respond positively, such as by sharing appreciation for your feedback or putting it into action, that gives you a window into what it might be like to share more consequential feedback with them next time.

Piling on more feedback to someone who has already received a lot of it isn't always helpful either. If a friend or colleague has already received negative feedback on something from multiple people, or if they are feeling upset about feedback they received, adding more on top of what they have already heard is unlikely to help. I'll share a personal example. Many years ago at work I made a snarky and unhelpful comment on a large conference call. As soon as I said it, I knew it was wrong. I felt really guilty and ashamed and regretful. I reached out to the person leading the call later that day and apologized for my actions. That person proceeded to give me a very direct talking-to about my comment, which I patiently listened to without defending or interrupting. It was a challenging and painful emotional experience for me, and it was then exacerbated by more negative feedback from several other colleagues. Every time another colleague gave me feedback on it (via conversation, email; sometimes skillfully, sometimes not) it was like re-opening the wound. I felt very self-aware about what I had done wrong and really didn't need to hear it from several more people. In situations where someone may have already heard the feedback several times *and* they are showing self-awareness and understanding, holding back and sharing support instead of feedback might be most helpful to them.

Another reason you might not share feedback is simply because the situation or relationship isn't that important to you. Because you are reading this book, I'm cognizant that you are responsible and conscientious (some of you might even identify as "over-functioners"), and so I want to give you permission to not feel like you always have to be responsible for holding up the mirror to other people. You might have an arsenal of data and observations about another person, but if the moment has passed, if you will never see them or work with them again, if you don't really think they will care about what you have to say, or if you simply lack the emotional and mental fortitude to have the conversation, sometimes it's okay to just not give the feedback. Choose your battles. Use your time and mental and emotional energy on the people and situations that feel most important to you. Consider having a go-to question to help you make those decisions, such as, "Will giving this feedback benefit me, my organization, or the recipient?" Or ask yourself, "What is the most likely best outcome from this feedback exchange?" One really important reason to not share feedback is if you do not have positive intentions. If you feel an urge to give feedback in order to "put the other person in their place," you and they will probably be better off if you do not share that feedback. This is why the first step in giving feedback— check your intention—is so important. Remember that feedback doesn't take place in a vacuum; all feedback occurs in the context of a relationship. Any feedback conversation will be colored by your prior interactions with that person and will also impact your relationship going forward.

You may give feedback to someone you have worked or been friends with for 20 years, and that relationship will continue for another 20 years. You may provide feedback to someone you barely know, after a brief interaction. A bad feedback exchange could signal the end of a relationship. Honest, helpful feedback could catalyze a relationship that will continue to grow. What you say, how you say it, and when you say it will elicit emotional and cognitive reactions from the feedback recipient that will shape not only how they perceive the feedback but also how they perceive you and the relationship that you share. Positive psychologist Barbara Fredrickson's (2013) research[3] has demonstrated that a positivity ratio of roughly 3:1, positive interactions/emotions to negative, leads to happiness, thriving, and strong relationships. Observe your feedback behavior with colleagues and family members over time: do your interactions and feedback conversations meet the 3:1 ratio? In other words, across all of your interactions with a given person, have you had 2–3 positive interactions to buffer against every instance of negative feedback? Every interaction that you have with someone shapes how they will react to and behave in your next feedback exchange, and that feedback exchange, in turn, will impact your future interactions. Recall that how the recipient perceives you, the feedback provider, impacts how they hear your feedback. If they believe you are credible, trustworthy, and know what you are talking about, they will be much more likely to accept and use feedback that you provide (Ilgen et al., 1979). Developing your own self-awareness will help you better regulate your behavior in these conversations. Using the best practices discussed in this chapter—making your feedback as specific as possible, being behavior-focused and evidence-based, using the Situation-Behavior-Impact (SBI) model, and providing feedback in a timely manner—is essential. By remembering that any feedback exchange is simply a human interaction, you can take your feedback skills to a higher level and build stronger, trust-based relationships through your exchanges.

Giving Feedback in Day-to-Day Life—What Will You Try?

Every day you are surrounded by opportunities to give either high-quality or thoughtless feedback or to choose to give or withhold feedback that could be potentially useful and eye-opening to others. I asked a few friends and colleagues what feedback situations they find most vexing. Here are some of my favorite responses, and my thoughts on how you might approach each situation using the best practices that we've covered in this chapter. Even if you're unlikely to find yourself in these exact situations, these examples may give you ideas for applying the techniques in your own life.

Giving Second-Hand Feedback

Often, leaders and managers find themselves in situations where they must communicate negative feedback second-hand to a member of their team. What I mean by second-hand is feedback that someone else provided or based on someone else's observations. This dynamic can occur during formal review processes, such as when a manager collects feedback from colleagues about a member of their team, and then integrates that feedback into their review. It can also occur in the day-to-day flow of work, if a manager has heard feedback from several people about a member of their team and feels a responsibility to have the difficult conversation. Providing second-hand feedback doesn't always enable the provider to follow feedback best practices. The provider may not have been in the situation where the behavior occurred and therefore did not see it with their own eyes. As a result, being evidence-based and specific can be challenging. Often, second-hand feedback is in regard to behavior that has taken some time to unfold or for people to speak up about, thereby making it hard to provide in a timely manner. Should you find yourself in this position, there are a few tools you can use to make the most of the situation. The first is to gather as much data and detail as possible from the people who are giving you the feedback, including pushing for specific behaviors. The second is to be really honest with the person you are providing feedback to, which could include sharing your own discomfort. This might sound like:

> Jenny, I have received feedback about your approach to making banana bread from several colleagues. I want to share with you some themes and patterns in the feedback. I want to note that I am not here when you are making banana bread, so this feedback is not based on my own observations. I think this feedback will be helpful to you, which is why I want to share with you what I have heard.

Third, as you can see in that example, you want to focus on sharing themes and patterns, then supporting those with specific examples. That shows the recipient that you aren't dwelling on a single piece of feedback that you heard, but on a pattern of behavior that you have become aware of. Finally, you might encourage the recipient to avoid playing the guessing game of "who said what" and trying to single out colleagues. Try to get them to focus on the impact of their behavior and what's important about the message. You might also consider working with the colleagues who provided you the feedback to help them develop their feedback skills and courage to share the feedback directly in the future.

Giving "Upward" Feedback to My Boss

Power differentials make feedback complicated. People may be inclined to withhold or water down negative feedback to recipients whom they perceive to be in a position of power over them. They may fear retaliation or doubt the validity of their observations. When giving upward feedback, follow the same feedback best practices that you would in any other scenario. You might simply need to work on your confidence and muster up the courage to say what's on your mind. Take the time to plan out what you want to say. Check your intentions and why you want to provide this feedback in the first place. Try sharing one piece of feedback and seeing how it lands, to determine if you would feel comfortable sharing more later. Many leaders live in a "feedback vacuum"—as they progress higher in their career, they have fewer superiors and peers to provide them with candid feedback (Hall et al., 1999). Yet managers and leaders need feedback to grow, develop, and have increased self-awareness as much as anyone else. Like the celebrity magazines would say: Bosses—*they are just like us!*

Giving Feedback to My Teenager in a Way That Doesn't Make Them Slam Their Door

I have spent hundreds of hours teaching, speaking, and leading workshops about coaching and feedback skills, and one of my favorite common observations from participants is that adopting a forward looking or coaching approach in conversations dramatically improves their communication with their teenage children. Recall that bringing a coaching approach means asking open-ended questions and giving the other person ownership for coming up with a solution. Next time you need to remind Khalil to put his shoes away, try giving him ownership and options for how he resolves the situation, rather than being directive. Rather than "Khalil, I told you to put your shoes away. Put them away now," try, "Khalil, when you leave your shoes in the middle of the living room floor it's really easy for others to trip over them. You can put your shoes anywhere you want, but out of the way. What would you like to designate as your shoe drop zone?" Notice the use of the SBI model here, followed by an open-ended question.

Giving a Meaningful Compliment

When your BFF landed her dream job, your coworker crushed his presentation, or your local baker made the best pastry you've ever tasted, use your feedback best practices to give a compliment that really means something. Humans are hard-wired to think about negative situations in more detail and think at a higher, more general level when things are going well (Bodenhausen et al., 1994). This often shows up in the feedback we give others. Whereas most people tend to be very detailed and specific in their negative feedback, positive feedback may be as general as "nice haircut," "great job on that presentation," or "Mmmm, this is delicious." Compliments can be much more powerful and meaningful and can help people identify good behaviors to repeat in the future when they follow feedback best practices—like being specific and behavior-based. Instead, of "congrats on your new job, Xena!" try, "Xena, you have worked so hard to develop as a leader and build your expertise in your field. You really earned this new role—I'm so proud of you!" Or "Aaron, your presentation this morning was well organized, making it clear and easy to follow. You tied a lot of details together into a compelling story that made your points memorable and high impact." And "Nelson, this cinnamon bun has the perfect consistency—it's crispy on the outside and gooey on the inside and has so much cinnamon flavor." Lastly, check the focus of your compliment. For example, say "Amir you look fantastic in that dress!" (compliment Amir) as opposed to, "Amir that dress looks so good on you!" (complimenting the dress).

Sharing Negative Feedback in Service Settings

You got a bad haircut . . . it feels easier to never go back to your hairstylist again than to share the critical feedback about their handiwork. Avoidance is always an option, but it doesn't fix the situation or help the other person learn or grow. Applying feedback best practices—being specific, focusing on observable behavior or outcomes, framing feedback in terms of behavior, not the person, and being forward-looking—will make those tough feedback conversations in service settings a bit easier. Next time your haircut (or other service) doesn't turn out the way you imagined, think about the outcome that would make you feel better—do you want your stylist to fix it now? To cut it differently next time? To offer you a refund? Having clarity on what "good hair" looks like will also help you ground your feedback. In Chapter 1, we learned that the real value of feedback is helping you gauge the distance between the current state and the desired state. So, if your current state (bad haircut) is far off from your desired state (good hair), what will it take to close that gap? And what is the timeline—is it today, or when you get your next haircut?

You can apply these same practices in other settings where the outcome isn't exactly what you were looking for—if your steak is overcooked at a restaurant, the clerk packs your bags too full at the grocery store, or if you feel like your primary care doctor isn't really listening to your questions and concerns. In that last example, you might say to your doctor,

> Dr. Schein, when I asked you a question earlier about changing my diet, your answer of "Oh, you're doing fine" didn't actually answer my question and made me feel dismissed. I want to proactively manage my health, and I would appreciate spending more time and attention on my questions, particularly since I only see you once a year.

Wrapping Up

We explored a lot of territory in this chapter about how to be a better feedback provider and give high-quality feedback that others can use to learn, grow, and have higher performance. We covered three steps to help you be more effective at giving feedback, which align with the three provider-focused elements of the feedback exchange: (1) clarifying your intention, followed by (2) planning what you say and how, where, and when you say it, and finally, (3) preparing yourself to be present and give the other person space to process what you have shared. We saw a variety of examples that have hopefully allowed you to see yourself in the role of feedback provider, leveraging best practices grounded in science. In the next chapter, we'll flip to the other side of the exchange and take a look at how to be a better feedback recipient.

Try It

Next time you need to give someone feedback and you're feeling uncomfortable or uncertain, try writing your feedback down. Read it over and see how you can make it more specific, evidence-based, and focused on behavior. Then, practice saying it out loud—saying what you need to say, then stopping. Make any necessary revisions, then say it out loud again. Maybe say it one more time, until you feel a little more comfortable delivering it to the recipient.

Pro Tip

Technology has its pros and cons when it comes to giving feedback, but one great use case is getting "feedback on your feedback" from AI to strengthen your message. Nicole Mehrhoff, HR Director at Bombas, shares that she

> encourages managers to use AI technology like ChatGPT to refine their feedback before delivering it. You can ask AI for suggestions on how to make feedback it more impactful and aligned to best practices, such as clarifying specifics, highlighting the impact, or refining the message. You can also get insight into how the tone might be received and ask for suggestions on how you can adjust accordingly to ensure your feedback is constructive and well-received.

Notes

1 Check out Appendix C for an SBI worksheet
2 Take a look at Appendix D for a worksheet you can use to set clear expectations with this framework.
3 The efficacy and replicability of Fredrickson's research have been called into question, but her 2013 article showed continued empirical support for the existence and importance of the positivity ratio.

Ask for It   4

In this chapter, we will

- Normalize that receiving feedback can feel difficult or daunting, and discuss specific strategies to make receiving feedback feel more manageable.
- Explore the important role of mindsets for receiving feedback, including three specific mindsets that you can choose to adopt.
- Take a look at three behaviors you can use to be a more effective feedback recipient in both formal and informal feedback conversations.

Imagine this scenario: you are sitting at your desk (or wherever you spend most of your days) and a colleague, friend, family member, or partner comes around the corner and says, "[Your name here], I need to give you some feedback." Close your eyes. Really imagine this situation. Use your best visualization skills. What does the setting look like? Who is the person giving you the feedback? Imagine their expression, their tone.

What's your immediate emotional reaction to their words?

If you are like many people, it's negative. In previous chapters, we saw that people respond to this statement with reactions like, "brace yourself," "get ready to hear something negative," "duck and wait for criticism." Often, people feel like feedback is *happening to* them. It's not something they asked for. It's presented at the time and place that's convenient for the provider, not when the recipient is ready, open, and interested in receiving the feedback. Unsolicited

DOI: 10.4324/9781003486510-4

critical feedback can make you feel powerless—as if the feedback provider holds all of the power and control in the situation.

Getting beyond reactions like dread, bracing, expecting the worst, or feeling hijacked requires a shift to an *ownership mindset* and a realization that, in any two-person feedback exchange, each person is 50% of the conversation. The powerless mindset of feeling like feedback is happening *to* you is likely shaped by years or decades of feedback interactions in which a person with power (a parent, teacher, coach, boss) approached feedback as a one-way, not-up-for-discussion transaction. Undoing the mindset that feedback *happens to* you requires a realization and acceptance that you ultimately have a choice in what you do with feedback that others provide to you. As is the case with most human interactions, you cannot control others' behavior, but you can control how you respond and what you choose to do with their actions or words. In London and Smither's (2002) classic model of the feedback process, the delivery of feedback, the choice to accept that feedback, and the decision to actually *do* something with the feedback are three very distinct steps, and the feedback recipient has full control over the last two—the choices to accept or use feedback.

In the last chapter, we focused primarily on the actions and choices of the feedback provider (and their implications). In this chapter, we will explore tools and strategies for being a better feedback recipient, including specific mindsets and behaviors that will lead to a more comfortable and satisfying feedback exchange; higher quality, more actionable feedback; and a feeling of being an active participant in the conversation, not a victim of the feedback. The best practices that we explore apply to both informal, day-to-day feedback, as well as more formal feedback settings. Near the end of the chapter, we'll discuss some of the challenges and choices you have in two common formal feedback situations: performance reviews and receiving 360 feedback. But first, let's examine three mindsets you can adopt and three behaviors you can use to be a better feedback recipient across the board, summarized in Figure 4.1.

Three Helpful Mindsets[1]

We've explored the importance of mindsets in Chapters 2 and 3. Recall that the attitude, expectations, and state of mind you bring to a feedback interaction will color your perceptions and

MINDSETS	BEHAVIORS
① ASSUME POSITIVE INTENT	① REALLY LISTEN
② HAVE PATIENCE WITH THE PROCESS	② ASK QUESTIONS
③ ADOPT AN OWNERSHIP MINDSET FOR YOUR 50% OF THE INTERACTION	③ PROACTIVELY ASK FOR FEEDBACK

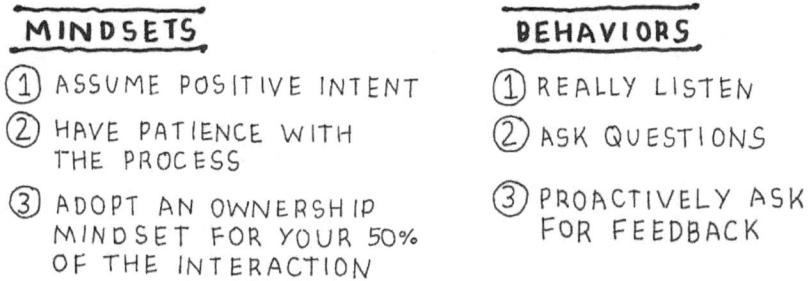

Figure 4.1 Three mindsets and three behaviors that make receiving feedback more effective.

influence your behavior. As I mentioned in Chapter 2, I like to think of adopting a mindset as selecting a pair of glasses that will impact how you are experiencing (or "seeing") a particular situation. In addition to these "in the moment" mindsets you can choose to adopt, you also have more pervasive mindsets, such as either a growth or fixed mindset, as well as your feedback orientation, which is your attitude toward feedback that impacts the way you think about, value, and use feedback, and whether or not you are inclined to seek it out (Linderbaum & Levy, 2010). Fortunately, your feedback orientation is not fixed, and with effort and exposure to effective feedback interactions, you can develop and strengthen your feedback orientation. This takes time, and it takes a growth mindset to believe that you can grow, learn, and change (Dweck, 2006). While you develop your feedback orientation in the long term, you can practice three very specific mindsets "in the moment" of any feedback exchange: assuming positive intent, having patience with the feedback process, and adopting an ownership mindset for your 50% of the interaction.

Assume Positive Intent

One strategy you can use to stay open and objective in feedback conversations is to assume positive intent in the feedback provider (Barnes et al., 2017). Assuming positive intent means you approach any interaction with the belief that the other person has your best interests at heart in their words and actions and are giving feedback because they genuinely want to help. The program Powerful Coaching by Results Coaching (2025) breaks the practice of assuming positive intent into three steps: (1) adopting the belief that the other person has positive intentions in all of their actions and behaviors, (2) presuming the other person has previously thought about what they are talking about, and (3) using language that indicates your positive assumptions about the other person's intentions. Practicing the assumption of positive intent can help you be more present and attentive in a conversation, because less of your cognitive resources are devoted to wondering what the other person really means or what their agenda is. It can also help you become more aware of your own biases, judgments, and assumptions about the other person; as these pop up in your mind, you can notice them and let them go in order to give the other person a chance to say what is on their mind, and then really listen to them. Research has shown that when you and the other person have shared goals, shared activities, and a strong relationship, or "bond," the assumption of positive intent naturally follows (Ajjawi & Regehr, 2019; Telio et al., 2016). Most likely, assuming positive intent will be more challenging in the presence of individuals with whom you do not have shared goals, activities, or a strong relationship.

The assumptions that we make about others' intentions or motivations color our perceptions of their behavior. If we assume ill intent, we automatically have our guard up, get defensive, and are skeptical of the motivation and agenda behind their words and actions. We enter a self-protective mode. Providing feedback to others can be an intimidating and uncomfortable experience for many providers. Because of this discomfort (and likely their lack of skill or preparation), a feedback provider may not articulate the feedback completely clearly or show the right degree of empathy or concern. They might talk too much, making the message unclear or talking themselves into a hole. They might fill silence with words that add no value. It's easy to interpret this awkward behavior as uncaring or ill-intended. However, if you assume positive intent, you give the feedback provider the benefit of the doubt: you assume that they really do care and are just doing a bad job of giving you feedback. Keep in mind that the other person is probably uncomfortable giving you feedback, and they are putting themselves into this uncomfortable position *because* they care about you and want to help you learn, grow, or uncover a blind spot. The truly uncaring person is the one who *doesn't* go out of their way to give you the feedback.[2]

Practice Patience With the Process and Yourself

You are hardwired to have an immediate emotional reaction to negative feedback. "Cool cognition" and rational thought take time to catch up with "hot emotion." You need to give yourself time to let the immediate emotional reaction pass before you can truly process and think clearly about the feedback. The sooner you recognize this, the easier all of your feedback interactions will be. Mindfully processing feedback that you receive is the gateway to doing anything productive with it (London & Smither, 2002). Back in Chapter 2, we saw that the process of receiving feedback can actually entail up to seven steps:

1. Hear or read the feedback.
2. Have an initial emotional reaction.
3. Process the feedback as rational thought catches up and emotions cool off.
4. Decide whether or not to accept the feedback.
5. Determine if anything is unclear or if you need more information.
6. Decide what to do next (have a follow-up conversation, dismiss the feedback, choose to act on the feedback).
7. Do something with the feedback.

The amount of time that you need to let your emotions unfold, allow cognition to catch up, and really process the feedback may vary based on the feedback, the situation, and your own patterns and tendencies (including your feedback orientation). Simply counting to ten may provide the time and space that you need to be able to process feedback. But more likely, you will need more time to process, in which case, a helpful course of action to ensure a productive outcome for you and the feedback provider may be to say, "*Thanks. I need to give this a little more thought. Do you mind if we reconnect later today or tomorrow morning to talk about next steps?*" Don't be afraid to be candid—"*This is a lot to process, and I feel like I need a little time and space to reflect on this feedback."* Once the emotion has passed and you're able to think more clearly about the feedback, remind yourself that you don't have to just blindly accept it. You have a range of choices in how you can handle the feedback. In Chapter 5, we'll focus on practices for acting on feedback and putting it to use.

In addition to understanding the role of emotion, cognition, and biology, remember that the attitudes and beliefs you have developed over the course of your lifetime also affect your feedback experiences. Recall that your feedback orientation—your overall attitude toward feedback—underlies how you feel about feedback (Do you love it? Hate it?), how much you value feedback and find it useful, and if you find it helpful for developing self-awareness (Linderbaum & Levy, 2010). Research has shown that a person's feedback orientation impacts how deeply they process the feedback, how they interpret and react to feedback, and the extent to which they do something with it (Katz et al., 2023; London & Smither, 2002). Although your feedback orientation has been shaped by years of past experiences, you can choose to invest in and develop your feedback orientation by intentionally choosing and learning to value, use, and seek out feedback. Although many aspects of our personality (i.e., who we are as people) are relatively stable over time, we can shift our attitudes and beliefs. Openly accepting feedback and using it to have higher performance will help you build self-efficacy and self-confidence over time, which, in turn, will make you more open to and assured about handling feedback in the future (Brown et al., 2001; Colquitt et al., 2000). Your current mood can also impact how you perceive feedback. Research has shown that feedback is more likely to be viewed as accurate when the sign of the feedback is congruent with the recipient's mood. For example, if you are in a negative mood when you enter a feedback interaction, you will view negative feedback as more accurate and be more inclined to process it deeply; when in a positive mood, we view positive feedback as more accurate (Hammer & Stone-Romero, 1996). Remember that negative feedback has a great deal of utility for helping us learn, grow, strengthen our performance, and become more self-aware, so allowing your mood to flex with the sign of the feedback can actually help you see it as more accurate and potentially as having more utility.

*Adopt an Ownership Mindset for Your 50% of
the Interaction*

In the years since writing the first edition of this book, I have spent hundreds of hours talking to people about feedback, delivering workshops on feedback, and learning about people's experiences with feedback. One of the biggest discoveries I have had from those experiences is seeing how often people struggle with a victim mindset when it comes to receiving feedback, this feeling that feedback is happening *to* them (among other things; see Figure 4.2 for examples). They do not feel like an equal participant in the conversation and don't always feel empowered to ask questions, have a dialogue, and decide what they want to do with feedback.

Feedback is not a one-way conversation, although many people seem to experience it that way. Although it may feel like the feedback provider is in full control and feedback is "happening to you," remember that you are 50% of the feedback exchange. You cannot control how skillfully (or unskillfully) the feedback is provided, when the provider chooses to share it, what medium they choose, or their precise words, but you do get to choose how you respond to and use the feedback, both in the moment and in the longer term. This ownership mindset might demand some other related mindsets from you. For example, you might benefit from adopting a mindset of courage, curiosity, or of seeing yourself as competent or resourceful. Each time you receive feedback is an opportunity to experiment with different ways of framing the conversation until you find one that makes you feel more like an equal participant and owner of your experience.

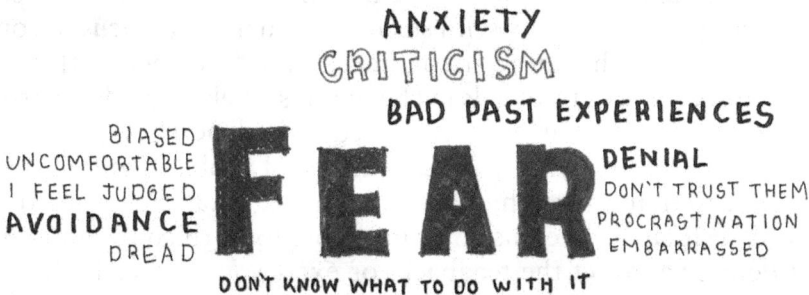

ANXIETY

CRITICISM

BAD PAST EXPERIENCES

BIASED
UNCOMFORTABLE
I FEEL JUDGED
AVOIDANCE
DREAD

FEAR

DENIAL
DON'T TRUST THEM
PROCRASTINATION
EMBARRASSED

DON'T KNOW WHAT TO DO WITH IT

Figure 4.2 Common reactions to anticipating feedback.

For example, Finch, the wealth manager we heard from in Chapter 2, recounted how she chose to stay calm, really listen, and seek to understand a client who gave her angry critical feedback. A misunderstanding had occurred between Finch's team and the client. The client was known for talking forcefully and having a temper. In this particular instance, he provided negative feedback in an unskillful way, criticizing the individuals on the team, yelling, and hanging up on a member of Finch's team. Finch proposed that they meet in person for a follow-up conversation. She anticipated that the conversation would be challenging, and she had developed rapport with this client over the years and was invested in maintaining their relationship and fixing the situation. During the conversation she listened, stayed calm, and managed her emotions. Not only did she hear and accept the client's feedback, she also turned the conversation into a collaborative dialogue by providing feedback to the client about his behavior. She shared that his feedback focused on members of her team personally, as opposed to specific actions or behaviors that he was unhappy with, and that raising his voice and talking for most of the conversation did not allow the team an opportunity to ask him questions and learn more about the situation so they could repair it. Even though the conversation was uncomfortable, it strengthened and changed the nature of their relationship to be less one-sided and with increased understanding between the two of them. Later the client shared with Finch that he respected the way she handled the situation by de-escalating it and even giving him feedback on his own behavior.

Staying calm and working through strong emotional reactions in challenging feedback exchanges is not easy. Accepting feedback with grace and cool emotions is easier if you have a strong feedback orientation, healthy self-esteem, and an internal locus of control,[3] all of which can be strengthened and developed with time and effort. In any feedback exchange, it's likely that the person giving you feedback is not well-versed in feedback best practices, is uncomfortable giving you feedback, and probably didn't take the time to think through, plan, and practice what they wanted to say. In a situation like this you can choose to be ruled by emotion, get defensive, reject the feedback, or exert your power by trying to make the feedback provider feel wrong or foolish or guilty. Alternatively, you can assume positive intent, listen objectively, seek to understand what they are trying to communicate to you, and exert your power in the situation by asking clarifying questions and turning the exchange into a dialogue. These contrasting approaches result in notably different outcomes for both people involved and for their relationship going forward. A feedback exchange that starts with discomfort and negative emotion can either escalate into a destructive and frustrating debate or evolve into a collaborative and productive dialogue, depending on the decisions and actions of both people involved. It's important to recognize that the direction of the conversation is in the hands of both the feedback provider and the feedback recipient. Again, you can't control how the other person gives you feedback, but you can control how you respond to it and what you do next.

In the next section, we'll explore three behaviors that you can practice to take more ownership for your feedback experience, but ultimately *success begins with you seeing yourself as an equal participant in the dialogue.* Research has shown that people are more likely to ask for feedback when they feel a sense of ownership for their work (or whatever the context/focus of the feedback) (Qian et al., 2015). Only you "own" your behavior and have the ability to choose what actions you will take based on the feedback you have received. Even if the person giving you feedback is in a significant position of power or authority, or if the feedback feels high stakes or intense, you always have a choice. The choice is much broader than "just accept it as is" or "reject it outright"—there are many shades in between. You can use the three behaviors described below to assert your 50% of the feedback exchange and make any feedback dialogue feel more productive.

Three Helpful Behaviors

Once your mind is in the right place, you can choose how you want to engage in the feedback discussion. If the feedback provider is highly skilled at delivering feedback, you may leave the conversation with clarity, feeling supported, encouraged, and with tangible next steps for action. However, if the feedback you receive is not entirely clear, provokes you, feels inconsistent with your own perceptions, or otherwise raises questions, you have many tools available to help you make the most of the interaction. Empathy goes a long way on both sides of the feedback exchange, and it is at the heart of the three behaviors covered here. When you are on the receiving end of feedback, you want the feedback provider to show empathy in their delivery. As a feedback recipient, you can use empathy to better understand the feedback provider's perspective if you don't entirely agree with their feedback. Try to take their perspective—what are they seeing that you are not seeing? How has their experience or perception of the situation differed from your own? It's easy to get caught in the trap of wanting to be "right" (or being sure that you *are* "right"); don't let your need to be right get in the way of understanding the other person's perspective. They may see or know something you don't yet. And it's impossible to truly understand the other person's perspective if you aren't really listening to them.

Really Listen

In Chapter 3, we learned about the importance of being fully present and *really* listening in order to be an effective feedback provider. Listening is even more important when you are on the receiving end of feedback. Listening to understand—not to react or respond—will enable you to gain a deeper understanding of the situation and what the other person is trying to tell you. Think about a recent experience you had as a feedback recipient. As the provider was talking, how deeply were you listening? Were you practicing open and objective listening, attempting to really hear and understand their feedback? Or were you simply "reloading" and thinking about all the things you wanted to say to prove why you were right and they were wrong, to justify or rationalize your behavior, or explain why that situation was a one-time exception? If you are thinking about how you want to respond, you are not truly listening. Recall that *really* listening means listening with your attention entirely on the feedback provider, seeking to understand their perspective and collect the data they are sharing with you (Whitworth et al., 2009).

Failing to pay full attention will lead you to miss subtle nuances in the provider's words, tone, expressions, and body language, all of which serve as important data points in the dialogue. Distractions such as technology or focusing on your "inner monologue" will inhibit you from being fully present and attentive, which are foundational for really listening. If you find yourself getting derailed by your own reactions to the conversation (e.g., feeling like feedback is unfair, disagreeing with a statement), use your powers of curiosity and empathy to stay focused. Get curious about what the other person is saying. Practice empathy and expand your understanding by considering possibilities like "I wonder why she feels that way?" or "How could he be seeing this situation differently than I am?" Then, listen carefully for the answers. This exercise will help you not only learn more but also stay present and focused in the discussion and not get distracted by your own inner monologue and immediate reactions.

Ask Questions

Questions can be your secret weapon in a feedback conversation. Questions invite more information and clear up potential confusion or misunderstanding, and they can also help you buy time and manage your emotions in a challenging feedback exchange. For example, during Rae's annual performance review, her manager gave perplexing feedback: "Rae, it's been a tough year and this just isn't working." Rae's immediate reaction is one of surprise and alarm—her feedback throughout the year had never led her to believe that things "aren't working." Rae felt her heart rate increase and her mind start to race (*"I'm not performing. I'm going to get fired. OMG, I don't want to look for a new job. What happened?"*). She took a few deep breaths and said to herself, *"I have no idea what she means—before I freak out, let me see what I can figure out."* Rae asks her manager, "Lee, can you tell me more? What exactly isn't working?" Rae pulled herself back from her emotional downward spiral and asked open-ended questions to draw out more information from her manager. As the conversation unfolded, Rae discovered it wasn't as bad as she thought. Her manager, Lee, was referring to one specific project where a complex team structure was holding back progress. But Lee kept most of that context in her mind and started the conversation with vague, general, sweeping feedback—the exact opposite of the specific, behavior-based feedback that actually drives learning and performance.

In this example, Rae's manager Lee failed to use feedback best practices. Rae could have let her immediate assumptions, reactions, and emotions take over and derail the conversation, but instead she exerted her 50% ownership of the conversation and asked open-ended questions to help Lee more effectively articulate her feedback. Open-ended questions are essential for moving feedback discussions forward. Unless the feedback provider is a true expert at providing feedback—someone who has practiced and prepared for the conversation—it's likely they will unintentionally leave out some information, gloss over a few important details, or fail to provide sufficient context. And in most cases, they mean no harm. It's only human for feedback to be imperfect. As a feedback recipient, you can choose to simply accept the feedback exactly as it is provided, despite potential holes, lack of clarity, or open questions. Or, you can choose to actively engage and advance the dialogue by asking clarifying questions, asking for examples, and inviting more information.

Open-ended questions are the backbone of deep inquiry practices, such as executive coaching. Executive coaches use open-ended questions (e.g., what, how, when questions; even "tell me more") to draw out their clients and help them think through a situation. As a feedback recipient, you can borrow this coaching technique to draw out more detail, information, and thinking from your feedback provider. Remember, the person providing feedback to you may be deeply uncomfortable and have difficulty fully explaining the issue. By asking them open-ended, curious questions (not questions meant to defend or interrogate), you will put them at ease, better understand the situation yourself, and change the tone of the conversation from potentially contentious or awkward to productive and collaborative. When you're ready to experiment, try using "what" questions rather than "why" questions, which can sometimes put the other person on the defensive. For example, Rae might really want to ask Lee, "Why is this relevant to me?" but she can reframe that question as "What about this is most important for me to be aware of?" If you were Lee, how would each of those questions land differently with you? The "why" question might make you feel like Rae is challenging you and that you have to justify your feedback; a simple reframe to a "what" question takes the temperature down and the pressure off and keeps the conversation moving forward in a productive direction.

As we learned in Chapter 3, one way to make feedback feel more constructive, to make the recipient less defensive, and to drive better future outcomes is to make the exchange forward looking. Recall the feedback conundrum: Feedback is by definition backward looking, which can sometimes lead us to feel powerless, deflated, and defensive since the moment may have passed and there's nothing we can do to go back and change it. However, as an active participant in the feedback exchange, you can ask a simple question to flip the lens of the feedback. In Rae and Lee's conversation, for example, Rae could ask, "Going forward, how can we change the composition of the team to improve the trajectory of this project?" or "What role can I play in this project to get it back on track?" This approach shifts the focus of the conversation away from rehashing the past and what's not working with the team, and into forward-looking, creative problem-solving mode. Although we know that advice is biased, asking for future-focused feedback can seem easier for the other person. They may feel like they are helping you do something different in the future, rather than criticizing you for something you've done in the past. You might ask a question like "If this situation were to arise again tomorrow, what's one thing you think I could do differently to result in a better outcome?" Although their answer will border on advice it's based on feedback about what happened last time. Discussing future behavior (either by asking a question or suggesting what you will do in the future) also shows the feedback provider that you have heard and understood their feedback and are considering ways to apply it.

Proactively Ask for Feedback

Finally, we get to asking for feedback. In feedback research, asking for feedback is usually referred to as *feedback seeking*. In Chapter 2, we briefly noted that proactively asking for feedback makes feedback both easier and more comfortable for the provider to give and for the asker to receive (West et al., 2018). For both parties, opening the door and inviting in feedback takes much of the anxiety and uncertainty out of the equation. People proactively ask for feedback for a variety of reasons and generally weigh the costs and benefits before asking (Ashford &

Northcraft, 1992). A whole body of research has focused on the various motives behind why people ask for feedback, and the impact of those motives on how they process the information and what they do with it (Anseel et al., 2018; Thoebes, 2024). These motives are often referred to as self-evaluation motives, and can be further broken into motives of self-improvement, self-assessment, self-enhancement, and self-verification (Sedikides & Strube, 1995). Self-improvement focuses on learning, growth, and getting data for a better future self, whereas self-assessment focuses on understanding how we're doing now. People who have self-improvement motivation genuinely want useful, constructive feedback to help them identify ways to improve their performance. On the other hand, self-enhancement and self-verification motives are all about protecting our self-concept, such as seeking positive feedback to make us feel better about ourselves or in an attempt to look good in front of others and be perceived in a positive light (Anseel et al., 2018; Ashford et al., 2003). People who seek feedback for self-enhancement purposes are more likely to perceive negative feedback as a threat (Thoebes, 2024). In fact, people may avoid asking for feedback as a means of self-preservation or ego defense, particularly in the presence of others. They don't want to feel criticized, or risk looking foolish or uncertain in front of others. Regardless of their motive, feedback seeking puts the recipient in the driver's seat, allowing them to control who gives them feedback, where and when they receive feedback, and what they want feedback on.

Several conditions increase the likelihood that people will actively seek out feedback. You'll recall from previous chapters that most people are uncomfortable receiving feedback in public. The same goes for feedback seeking: people are significantly more likely to ask for feedback in private settings (Williams & Johnson, 2000). Even if they have intentions of asking for feedback, once people enter a public setting, they will reconsider their intentions and either modify their question or hold back entirely. They weigh the costs and benefits of asking for feedback in public (such as the possible negative impact on how they are perceived by onlookers). "*Will I appear unsure, inadequate, or stupid if I ask this question?*" Regardless of the setting (public vs. private), people are also more likely to ask for instrumental feedback (i.e., feedback to help them improve their performance, not just make them look good or feel good) when they are working on some-thing new, when the task involves uncertainty, or when they are in the midst of change (Ashford et al., 2003).

Not all feedback sources are created equal when it comes to asking for feedback. Recall that feedback is much more likely to be accepted when it comes from a trustworthy and credible source. When the feedback recipient decides who to ask for feedback, they get to be selective and focus on sources who have cultivated that trust and credibility with them. Supportive, transformational leaders are significantly more likely to be asked for feedback than their more transactional counterparts[4] (Levy et al., 2002). A leader who only provides critical feedback without the foundation of a trusting relationship may soon find their direct reports engaging in "FAB"—feedback avoidance behavior (Moss & Sanchez, 2004), which occurs when people actively avoid situations or interactions that might lead to receiving feedback.

Being intentional about who you ask for feedback, when you ask for it, and what it will cover will impact the quality of the feedback and the conversation. For instance, let's say you pursued a decades-long dream of opening a private dog park that has a bar and food menu for dog parents, called Perro Pub. Before the grand opening, you might ask a few trusted friends and their dogs to spend an afternoon there and give honest and detailed feed-back about various aspects of their experience. You will likely get more helpful, more specific, and perhaps more honest feedback from these trusted friends than from the first-time patrons or online reviews. Proactively asking for feedback here might sound like

> Hey friends—I am about to launch Perro Pub in a few weeks and I would really like to get some advanced feedback so we can make any tweaks or catch any issues before our grand opening. Would you and your dog be willing to spend a few hours at the dog park and bar free of charge and give me feedback on your experience? Specifically, I want any feed-back—positive or negative—that you have on parking, entry, pricing and membership, the various dog play areas, the dog amenities (toys, water, treats), the human bathrooms, our beverage selection, and our food items, as well as anything else that you notice or wish we offered. When you visit, I will

give you a list of specific things I'm curious about and also want to hear any other feedback you have on your visit.

This example also relates to one of my favorite tools for feedback seeking, something I call the "pre-ask." The feedback pre-ask is when you ask someone in advance, before the situation even occurs, to carefully notice and pay attention to your behavior and give you feedback afterward. Once again, the more specific your question is, the easier it will be for providers to know what to focus on and later give you high-quality feedback. For example, if you are working on developing your presentation skills, you might say to a colleague, "Vivek, I am working on giving more focused, concise, and impactful presentations. In my presentation to the finance team this Thursday, could you pay attention to how I deliver my presentation and give me some feedback afterward?" Because feedback is by definition backward looking, feedback seeking usually takes place after something has occurred, which would look like asking Vivek for feedback *after* you deliver the presentation; with the pre-ask, you give Vivek a heads-up *before* the presentation so he can be intentional and attentive during your presentation and take the time to prepare his thoughts before your feedback conversation.

When, how, who, and what you ask for feedback on all impact the quality of the feedback provider's response. Giving the feedback provider time to think about your question and respond is likely to result in higher quality feedback. For instance, using the pre-ask allows them to notice, pay attention, and formulate a thorough response. You can also try using different communication channels, such as emailing your question to the person you want feedback from, then asking to have a conversation about it a few days later (you aren't necessarily asking them to send their feedback back to you in an email, you are just sharing your questions ahead of time so they have a chance to think about what they will share with you). The specificity of your question impacts the specificity and usefulness of the feedback you will receive in return. One of the least helpful questions you can ask when soliciting feedback is, "Can you give me some feedback?" Imagine being on the receiving end of that question: You don't know what the other person wants feedback on or what they are hoping to achieve. It is so broad that it's very difficult to answer. Instead, specific questions direct the focus of the feedback provider to ensure you get higher quality feedback in return. In our example of asking Vivek for feedback, we told him what we are looking for feedback on (our presentation skills), shared some context ("I am working on giving more focused, concise, and impactful presentations"), and even told him when and where we want him to observe our behavior ("In my presentation to the finance team this Thursday"). The key takeaway here is: When asking for feedback, a specific, focused question will get you more specific, focused feedback in return.

Feedback seeking isn't always this overt—in fact, we engage in a subtle form of feedback seeking every day. *Monitoring* is a form of feedback seeking where individuals do not actively ask for feedback but pay close attention to others' behavior and comments to pick up on feedback about their own performance and behavior (Williams & Johnson, 2000). For example, if you were giving that presentation to the finance team and noticed everyone in the room looked bored, were frowning, multitasking on their phones, or getting up and leaving the meeting, you might interpret these behaviors as negative feedback on your presentation. You didn't overtly ask for feedback from these individuals, but through monitoring you interpret their behaviors and expressions as feedback on how you are doing. David, the musician and producer we met in Chapter 1, uses monitoring extensively in live performances:

> Live performances are a total feedback festival. If things are going well on tour and in live shows, you go out on stage and receive massive positive feedback from hundreds or thousands of people showing that they appreciate your work. Body language is such valuable feedback—people can say any words, but their posture and body really tell the true story. We've had shows where the crowd is looking at their phones or you see a lot of folded arms, talking, or a couple yawns, and it's pretty tough. That's when you realize how much you depend on that unspoken feedback from the crowd to perform.

One risk with monitoring is that you might incorrectly interpret someone's behavior. In the example of the finance presentation, maybe people looked bored and tired because your presentation was right after lunch, or after several attendees had recently returned from a work trip to Japan and had bad jetlag. Perhaps people in the room crossed their arms and hunched in their chairs because the thermostat was set on 62 degrees and they were uncomfortably cold. Monitoring can be a useful source of data, but it is also prone to misinterpretation or misattribution.

The Try It exercise at the end of Chapter 1 invited you to pick a day and notice all of the feedback exchanges that you encounter. Have you tried it yet? How many examples of monitoring were included on your list? While directly asking others for feedback can be a more efficient and certain route for feedback, monitoring can provide some cues and clues to help us adapt our behavior and shape the questions we want to ask.

Making the Most of Formal Feedback

Much of this book has focused on informal, day-to-day feedback: feedback that is provided between individuals during the course of routine work and daily life. In my list of 25 instances of feedback that I recorded in a single day (Chapter 1), you may have been surprised by how basic and mundane most of the examples were. If so, you're not alone. When most people think of feedback, they think of formal, "event-based" feedback—such as an annual performance review (DeNisi & Pritchard, 2006; London & Smither, 2002; Pulakos & O'Leary, 2011). And those big feedback "events" can be especially stressful and anxiety-provoking. Many of the same feedback best practices we have discussed so far apply equally to both formal and informal settings, but there are some other situation-specific considerations that come with formal feedback exchanges. Let's take a look at the most daunting of them all first: performance reviews.

Performance Reviews

The experience of receiving formal feedback can feel different from day-to-day informal feedback, and annual performance reviews at work are one of the best examples. Feedback provided in an annual formal process tends to take the form of outcome feedback. It tells the recipient a summation of their performance for the year and is likely to be tied to important administrative processes like compensation, promotion, annual goal setting, and in some cases even reductions in force or other threats to job security. Receiving negative feedback in a performance review can be challenging because the opportunity for redemption may not exist. Let's go back to our example of Rae's performance conversation with her manager Lee: If Rae received a "needs improvement" rating, sure, she can make huge strides in the year to come, but that will not undo the disappointing rating she received this year, which is likely to remain in her employee record for the foreseeable future. Looking back to Chapter 2, we learned that this kind of negative outcome feedback is the least likely to drive future feedback seeking or performance improvement. In a disappointing formal review, emotional reactions may be even stronger than the already high emotional response that formal feedback exchanges can evoke. For instance, in a study of their performance management process, researchers at the software company Adobe (2017) found that 34% of millennial employees cried after their performance review and 47% started looking for new job opportunities.

Emotional reactions to formal events like annual reviews can be extreme (strong negative emotions in response to disappointing reviews; strong positive emotions in response to exemplary reviews), but many of the practices discussed throughout this chapter apply for maximizing the feedback dialogue in these high-stakes exchanges—such as truly listening and asking questions to clarify and understand. Remembering that you are 50% of the feedback exchange is important for formal reviews, too: Research has shown that people have stronger negative reactions to performance reviews when they feel like they were not actively involved in the process (Cawley et al., 1998). These strong emotions take time to pass, so a follow-up conversation a few days or weeks later to discuss next steps and implications can be effective. Even after a fabulous, positive review, it is tempting to bask in the glow of the great feedback and rewards, but once that initial glow has passed, try to think mindfully about how your high performance can be repeated (or accelerated) in the year to come.

Recall the trick we shared in Chapter 2 that you might use to make annual review feedback feel more developmental: reframe it as process, rather than outcome, feedback. Seeing your annual review feedback as entirely outcome-focused might sound like "Well, that's it. That's my evaluation for the year and there's nothing I can do about it. It is what it is." This interpretation is not very conducive to growth, development, and continuous improvement. If, instead, you told yourself, "Well, I have been here for three years and I have grown and advanced a lot. I see myself being at this organization for several more years, so this is just more data along the way on this 7-to-10-year journey." This simple reframe turns what may otherwise feel like outcome feedback into process feedback, or feedback *along the way*. You can use your year-end review feedback to inform your development and performance goals for the year ahead, focusing on the overall arc of your career with this organization, rather than simply the year that just concluded. Framing and reframing are helpful tools that you can use to make sense of feedback or experiences in a way that feels useful and productive for you. Even if you have a disappointing annual review, where the feedback isn't what you expect and your feedback provider isn't following best practices, you can choose how you frame the experience (not unlike choosing a mindset). On one hand, you might say, "This is a stupid process, and my boss is a jerk," but on the other hand, you could reframe this as "Let me see what useful nuggets of information I can pull out of this review to help me be even more successful in the year ahead."

I don't want to discount that sometimes reviews *are* unfair and sometimes bosses *are* jerks. I'm not encouraging you to acquiesce to bad circumstances, but rather to choose how you want to approach a situation to continue practicing that ownership mindset and extracting whatever value you can. You always have a choice about what you do with feedback you receive. If you believe that feedback is unfair and biased, consider your options: Is there actually some useful information in your review, even though your manager may be a jerk who is bad at giving feedback? Who is someone you trust and who will be honest with you that you could discuss the feedback with? Does your organization have a formal process for raising concerns about the fairness and equity of your review? Do you have an advocate, such as an HR partner, ombud, mentor, or former manager who you could discuss your experience with? Or maybe, is it time to look for a new role? The point is: don't forget that you always have choice about accepting the feedback, deciding what to do with it, having additional conversations to gather more data or learn more, or letting it signal to you that you want to make some other changes in your circumstances.

360 Feedback

Surveys and assessments also provide valuable formal feedback. Many organizations use 360-feedback assessments as a formal method for gathering feedback from multiple providers, including leaders/managers, peers, direct reports, and clients, to help employees get a holistic picture of their behavior or performance and how they are perceived by others. These 360 raters are typically invited to provide anonymous feedback that is aggregated and compared to the employee's self-ratings on the same dimensions. In a 360-feedback assessment, numerically rated questions (such as those scored on a 1- to 5-point scale ranging from "Strongly Disagree" to "Strongly Agree" or "Not at All" to "To a Great Extent") may tie back to an organizational leadership framework or competency model and also include open-ended questions where raters can provide qualitative feedback on what the recipient is doing well and what they are not doing well. 360-feedback tools are popular; one estimate showed that 85% of Fortune 500 companies use some kind of 360 tool (Forbes Business Insights, 2025). Research has shown that 360-feedback recipients usually find the feedback to be accurate and useful for helping them become more self-aware and make changes in their behaviors (Nurudeen et al., 2015).

360 (or "multisource") feedback provides a reality check by comparing our self-perceptions with the perceptions of others. Research has demonstrated an inverse relationship between performance and self-ratings, such that high performers tend to underrate their abilities while underperformers overestimate their abilities (Atkins & Wood, 2002). 360 feedback is a uniquely valuable form of feedback that enables individuals to examine their self-perceptions against the perceptions of others, often through helpful visuals like bar charts or graphs that highlight disconnects (or consistencies). The gaps between self-ratings and the ratings of others highlight important differences

in what people think of themselves and how they are perceived. For instance, when someone rates themselves more highly than others rate them, this might reveal some blind spots or an inflated estimate of one's capabilities, or it might indicate where raters are not getting enough exposure to the individual's strengths. On the other hand, when someone rates themselves consistently lower than others rate them, this might be the result of being overly self-critical or of raters inflating their ratings. It's also common to see variations in ratings or feedback across different raters or rater groups. It could be that the recipient behaves differently with certain people or in particular situations (e.g., peers vs. direct reports), or that their self-perceptions are harsher or more lenient than others' perceptions. Gaps such as these that are surfaced in 360s open important doors for the recipient to develop better self-awareness.

Participating in a 360-feedback exercise can drive higher performance, under the right conditions. Not surprisingly, behavior change and improved performance are most likely to occur when a 360 report contains a few specific, negative, behavior-based pieces of feedback (Smither & Walker, 2004). Receiving a large quantity of negative feedback, however, can feel overwhelming and lead to a decline in performance following the 360-feedback exchange. Large quantities of predominantly negative feedback can leave the recipient feeling deflated, demoralized, and unsure where to begin. Certain characteristics or individual differences of the feedback recipient make behavior change more or less likely, as well. One meta-analysis of longitudinal multisource feedback studies found that improvements in performance are most likely to follow 360 feedback when the recipient has a strong feedback orientation, believes that they can change,[5] perceives a need for change, is high on conscientiousness (one of the Big 5 personality variables[6]), and is goal oriented and effective at setting goals (Smither et al., 2005). Changes in performance attributed to participating in a 360-feedback assessment tend to be small and gradual. Behavior change is hard, after all.

360 feedback allows recipients to calibrate their behavior against others' standards, but the feedback provided by ratings alone may be insufficient. Ideally, qualitative feedback or comments in the 360-feedback report will help to explain some of those gaps, but these reports will rarely be exhaustive. When receiving a

360-feedback report, recipients may be tempted to quickly scan over it, looking for surprises, such as dimensions where they are rated highest or lowest, or where they see the biggest gaps between their self-ratings and others' ratings. But even the shortest 360 report is dense, with rich data points reflecting many perspectives, and may raise more questions than it answers. To extract the most value from a 360 report, an individual may want to give it a read, then put it away and look at it again a few days later with fresh eyes. An individual's mood and mindset at the time of reading the report can also influence their perceptions of the feedback and what they take away from it. As with all feedback, rather than being an "end product," a 360-feedback report is best considered the starting point for important follow-up dialogue. This is where the importance of asking questions about your feedback enters the picture. Research has also consistently shown that working with a coach or facilitator to review and make sense of 360 feedback results in better outcomes, something we'll examine more closely in Chapter 5.

Wrapping Up

By proactively asking others for feedback, you can lay the foundation for an effective feedback exchange. You can choose the context for the feedback: you can choose to ask in person, on the phone, or in writing to control the medium. You can ask in public or in private. You can ask immediately after something happens or wait until you're ready and have some distance from the event. You can ask questions that invite behavior-focused (as opposed to you-focused) and specific feedback. You can invite future-focused feedback by asking questions like "What is one thing I might do differently next time to be even more effective?" The simpler and more specific your question is, the easier it will be for the other person to respond. Remember, feedback providers may be just as intimidated and uncomfortable as you are. You can make feedback feel more comfortable and manageable for them by asking clear and focused questions.

One of the things I find most useful and interesting about feedback is that it tells you about yourself relative to the world around you. Without feedback we would operate in a vacuum. In a scene in the film *The Aviator*, Howard Hughes (Leonardo DiCaprio) forces a reshoot of a wild flight sequence because the sky was too clear. In the first take there were no clouds, no buildings, just planes and blue sky—no reference points. As a result, the viewer would be unable to fully discern how fast the planes were flying, or how bold and risky their maneuvers were. Reshot with clouds in the sky, suddenly the scene was more exciting and suspenseful. The clouds provided reference points that enabled the viewer to understand the real impact and detail of the pilots' actions. Think of feedback as the distance between those planes and clouds. It helps us understand how others see us, where we stand with respect to our goals, successes, and failures, and reflects information back to us about ourselves in the world. When it comes to being a great feedback recipient, stay open and seek to learn and understand the other person's perspective. Listen, ask questions, make the most of the exchange, even if the provider botches it. But ultimately, the decision is yours on what to do with the feedback they provide. You are 50% of the feedback exchange, and once feedback is given to you, you own the next steps. Accept feedback with grace, give yourself time to really process it, and then choose the best course of action to help you learn, grow, and achieve higher performance.

Try It

Today or tomorrow, ask someone for feedback. Ask anyone about whatever is on your mind. Ask a colleague, a friend, your partner, your kids, a fitness instructor. Ask for feedback in a way that makes it easy for them to respond and increases the likelihood you'll get useful feedback in return. Need a little help with this one? Try this feedback fill-in-the-blank:

> [*Person's name*], I'm looking for some feedback on [*my performance, a project, last night's dinner, my tennis backhand, whatever*]. Based on your observations, what's one thing that I did well and one thing that wasn't as strong as it could have been?

Pro Tip

After reading the first edition of this book, Mel Baxter, Founder & CEO of The Mel Baxter Group, shared with me her biggest takeaway:

> Understanding that I am 50% of every feedback exchange changed my perspective on feedback discussions. When I received feedback in the past, I frequently felt like the victim of a challenging conversation. Since reading the first edition of *Feedback Fundamentals*, I actively ask questions when receiving feedback. Doing so helps me better understand where the other person is coming from and brainstorm ideas for future improvement.

What do you need to do to also feel a sense of ownership for your experience receiving feedback?

Notes

1 Here, "mindsets" refers to the beliefs, attitudes, and expectations that influence how we perceive our experiences. In her work on "mindset," Carol Dweck (2006) focuses specifically on growth versus fixed mindset, which is an example of one set of attitudes or beliefs that people can have about their abilities.

2 Certainly, there's always a chance you will encounter a selfish or deviant colleague or friend who *does* intend to harm or make you feel bad with their feedback. When you encounter someone who truly has negative intent, consider asking yourself: What is driving their ill intentions? Is it about you, or is it really about them attempting to exert power, make themselves feel better or superior, or projecting from some other inter-action? Approaching these interactions from the same place of empathy and seeking to understand the feedback will help you navigate them without surrendering your own power in the interaction.

3 Having an *internal* locus of control means that you believe you can control your experiences and what happens to you. Having an *external* locus of control means you believe that things are happening to you and are out of your control. An internal locus of control has consistently been linked to positive outcomes—such as success in school and work, an achievement orientation, better health, higher self-confidence and

self-esteem, and seeing a direct effect between your hard work and effort and desirable outcomes, among other things.

4 Transformational leaders rely on inspiration and a shared vision, tailoring their approach to what motivates and grows the people they work with. In contrast, transactional leaders focus on a shorter time horizon and leverage rewards and punishments to drive people's behaviors, among other qualities that tend to harm employee growth. To learn more check out the book *Transformational Leadership* by Bernard Bass and Ronald Riggio (2006).

5 Specifically, these recipients have a strong incremental Implicit Person Theory, which means they believe that people are capable of change (similar to a growth mindset from Carol Dweck's research).

6 The Big 5 Theory of personality is one of the most widely used and accepted models of personality. In addition to conscientiousness, the Big Five dimensions include neuroticism/emotional stability, extraversion/introversion, openness to experience, and agreeableness (McCrae & Costa, 1987).

Use It   **5**

In this chapter, we will

- Acknowledge that putting feedback to use is hard, but not impossible.
- Outline five steps for taking action on feedback.
- Further connect the dots between goals, feedback, and behavior change.

Once you have gone through the process of hearing and deciding to accept feedback, the next step is to put it to use. Translating feedback into next steps, behavior changes, or ideas for experimentation isn't easy, but feedback that is specific, behavior-focused, and evidence-based is easier to put into practice than feedback that is vague and person-focused. Ideally, people give feedback because they want to see you do more of some behavior, do less of another behavior, or do some other behavior entirely. You'll recall that feedback providers are comparing your current behavior to some goal or standard—which could be explicit (an expectation they and/or you are aware of) or implicit (some expectation in their mind that perhaps neither of you is fully aware of). As a feedback recipient, you ultimately have a choice about what you will do with feedback. When feedback is positive and indicates that you are doing great work and are on track with goals and expectations, you might feel less like you're faced with a decision about what to do next. You'll probably feel a shot of positive

DOI: 10.4324/9781003486510-5

emotion and confidence in your work, then you'll go about your business as usual. People adapt very quickly to good news and gains and quickly revert back to their "typical" behaviors, a concept known as the hedonic treadmill.[1] Negative feedback, however, presents many options for deciding how to respond to it and what to do with it (Taylor et al., 1984). After receiving negative feedback (and getting through your immediate emotional reaction), you could choose to accept it at face value and immediately put it to use by adjusting your behavior. You could opt to dig deeper into it to understand the issues by asking questions or asking others for their perspective. You could choose *not* to accept it. Or you could think about it for a while and decide later (which could be driven by avoidance or wisely and intentionally postponing a decision). Even in situations where you may feel like you don't have a choice but to accept the feedback, you *always* have a choice about what you do with it.

An important part of deciding what to do with feedback is seeking to find the nuggets of useful information in the feedback message and prioritizing what you want to carry forward and what you want to leave behind for now. For example, although indirect feedback (such as online reviews left by customers) may be frustrating for businesses, the themes and patterns that emerge from aggregating consumer feedback in online reviews can highlight important needs and opportunities. One study found that Yelp reviews of hospitals uncovered important dimensions of patient care that hospitals were not evaluating (Ranard et al., 2016). The researchers found that Yelp reviews were highly correlated with traditional patient feedback surveys ($r = 0.50$) and also discovered 12 new categories that were not included on those traditional surveys, such as the cost of the hospital visit, staff compassion, care for visiting family members, the experience with billing and insurance, scheduling, and facilities, among other things. In short, reviewing indirect feedback, such as online comments, in aggregate (to avoid over-indexing on individual, dissatisfied customers) can help businesses identify criteria and dimensions that are important to consumers that they are not currently attending to. Ultimately, you want to be able to clearly identify what exactly it is that you are doing or not doing. What are the data about your behavior? You want clarity on what you are doing or not doing so you can decide what you want to do to address your behavior going forward.

In this chapter, we will break down the process of putting feedback to use into a few sequential steps, including (1) deciding what to do with the feedback, (2) identifying the gap you want to close (which includes goal setting), (3) breaking goals down to feel more manageable, (4) experimenting with behavior change, and (5) getting support from others. Asking for and receiving feedback can feel daunting, but sometimes the greatest challenge is figuring out what to actually do with feedback once you have accepted it. The goal of this chapter is to demystify that process and make it feel a little easier.

Decide What to Do With Feedback

Chapter 4 emphasized that the feedback recipient is 50% of any feedback exchange. When someone provides you with feedback, you "own" the decision about what to do next. Some situations may feel more empowering than others—when your iPhone gives you feedback about your screen time (see Figure 5.1), you might feel more discretion about what to do with that feedback compared to high-stakes performance feedback from your boss, but the truth is that both situations present you with options. You have a range of choices about what to do next. If you find the feedback to be accurate, helpful, and specific enough to immediately put to use, you may feel comfortable accepting it outright. For example, negative process feedback—that which tells

SCREEN TIME

WEEKLY REPORT AVAILABLE
YOUR SCREEN TIME WAS UP 32%
LAST WEEK, FOR AN AVERAGE
OF 3 HOURS, 44 MINUTES A DAY.

Figure 5.1 When your iPhone gives you feedback on your screentime, it's not judging you. But it is providing useful data.

you something you can do better or differently to get closer to your goals—can be applied right away and allow you to adjust or course correct in whatever you are working on (Earley et al., 1990; Medvedeff et al., 2008). Many feedback exchanges are not so straightforward and simple. You may need time and space to overcome an immediate emotional reaction and think mindfully about the feedback, or you may need to ask follow-up questions to really understand the issue, why it matters, and what you will do about it.

Christopher, the alumni team member of the non-profit Back on My Feet, who we first met in Chapter 1, has learned with time how to manage his emotional reactions to feedback. He has learned to find the nuggets of value in feedback, which in the past he would have simply reacted to and disregarded. Here's how he summarizes the approach he uses now:

> With training and practice, I've learned that I get to decide in a situation what I will do with feedback from others. I've learned that I have more options that just reacting. Instead of responding with frustration and anger, I can step back and make a conscious decision about what I want to do with the feedback. I've realized that I need to take time and recognize my feelings, not just immediately react, because nine times out of ten I would typically have a negative reaction, such as a fight or flight response. Now, I take a pause to practice empathy. I recognize that I don't always know what is going on with the other person or what they might be dealing with that I can't see. I recognize that they are only human, too.

Taking the time to pause, let your immediate emotional reaction pass, and think mindfully about the feedback will also help you identify missing details or formulate follow-up questions to make the feedback more useful and easily translatable to new behaviors. Recall Kluger and DeNisi's (1996) Feedback Intervention Theory (FIT) from previous chapters, which highlights the importance of *levels of abstraction* for translating feedback into behavior change. Feedback is much easier to act on when it is evidence-based and specific (a lower level of abstraction than broad generalizations) and focused on behavior rather than the person. And, if you don't receive feedback that checks those boxes, asking specific, open-ended questions will help you get more helpful data. In the hours or days after the immediate feedback exchange, asking for additional opinions or finding additional evidence to support or negate the feedback is another way to assess the value and relevance of feedback as you are deciding what to do with it. One reason 360-feedback assessments are so valuable is because they offer an array of perspectives and do not disproportionately emphasize one voice or one person's perspective. If someone provides feedback and you aren't sure if it's accurate or useful, find some other people you trust and ask for their opinion. Research has consistently shown that feedback is deemed more valuable when it comes from a credible source—someone the recipient sees as having expertise on the issue—and is trustworthy (Albright & Levy, 1995; Ilgen et al., 1979; Taylor et al., 1984; Vancouver & Morrison, 1995). Leverage your best practice feedback-seeking skills by asking open-ended, specific questions that enable others to feel comfortable giving you specific, constructive feedback.

Getting additional opinions or looking for patterns in feedback can provide a balanced perspective and ensure the feedback is not simply a reflection of one person's preferences or expectations. For example, Alex, the restaurant manager we met in previous chapters, pays close attention to customer reactions, behavior, and feedback anytime a new dish is on the menu:

> If a dish is not finished or is pushed to the side, we always ask for feedback on it. The absence of feedback is also meaningful because people usually comment positively on the dishes they love. So, if people are consistently NOT saying good things about a dish—that's meaningful feedback. It's not impressive and memorable enough. We look for patterns, and ask ourselves, is this feedback a one-off and simply attributable to one person's preferences? If I hear the same comment three times, that is meaningful, and we will act on it.

In Alex's example, calibrating the feedback is what ultimately drives their team to use or ignore feedback. If several different customers say that a dish is too salty, the kitchen accepts that feedback and adjusts the level of seasoning. However, if the guest at Table 20 believes the dish is too salty and everyone else who eats the same dish that night raves about it, the kitchen rejects or ignores the feedback from the guest at Table 20. Deciding what feedback to take on and what to ignore can be challenging. It requires some level of calibration and also a frame of reference for where the other person is coming from. In Chapter 1, David shared the example about another musician who he consistently disagrees with. When that friend gives feedback that he doesn't like a new piece that David plays for him, David actually knows he's on track. Although David is essentially rejecting the friend's feedback, he is able to interpret it as positive feedback since he knows they don't see eye to eye. Choosing to accept and act on feedback opens the door to a host of activities, like goal setting, behavior change, adopting or abandoning habits, self-reflecting, and even asking for more feedback to track your progress. One question I hear often in workshops is: what do I do if I give someone feedback and they aren't doing anything with it? Take a look at Box 5.1 for more.

Box 5.1 What if Someone Isn't Using My Feedback?

You gave someone feedback . . . and they aren't using it.

This chapter is all about putting feedback to use after receiving and accepting it. But what about times when you give someone feedback and notice that they don't seem to be using it?

As we have emphasized throughout the book, once you have given someone feedback, they own the decision about what to do with it: whether they choose to accept or reject it, how they respond to it, and whether or not they do anything with it.

If you have put yourself in the uncomfortable position of giving someone feedback, seeing them continue with the same behavior can be really frustrating. You may feel unheard, dismissed, or confused. You can't control that they haven't done anything with it, but you can control whether or not you address it again.

In this situation, you will once again want to draw on your feedback best practices to hold up the mirror and share data. That might sound something like, "Alice, two weeks ago in our 1:1 meeting I shared feedback with you about showing up late to sales meetings. Since our conversation, I have noticed that you came late to five of our last seven sales meetings."

A curious question could turn this into a dialogue, such as:

"What support do you need to get there on time?" or
"Help me understand what's getting in the way?"

A clear expectation shares the standard you're comparing their behavior to, such as being on time: "We have a shared agreement on our team that we show up on time and stay for the whole meeting, barring exceptional circumstances. I would like for you to get to the meetings on time or let me know if something is getting in the way, and how I can help."

Remember that you don't know what is going on in the recipient's brain, and you probably don't know the full picture of whatever they are experiencing. There is a chance that they really did process the feedback and they *do* want to do something with it, but haven't figured out how to get started. Bringing the feedback up with them once again could provide an opening to have a helpful conversation.

Identify the Gap You Want to Close

One of the reasons I personally love feedback is that it can provide a roadmap for closing gaps between our current state and desired state. And research has shown that I'm not alone: feedback is more likely to be accepted when we think it has informational value that will help us close the gap between where we are and where we want to be (London & Smither, 2002; Taylor et al., 1984), which is a core premise of control theory. Applied to one of our earlier examples, in a successful restaurant, the goal is for guests to leave happy and satisfied with their experience. You want them to enjoy every dish that they eat (goal/desired state). If the *current state* of their experience is dissatisfaction with an overly salted dish, their *feedback* on that dish helps the kitchen identify the gap between the current state and the goal state. Based on their feedback the action required to *close that gap* is adding less salt to the dish.

When feedback illuminates a gap between a current state and a desired state, there are two ways to close that gap. One choice is to adjust the current state to get closer to the goal or desired state. For example, if Josie has a goal of getting As in every class this year, but her midterm report shows she is tracking toward mostly Bs, one way she can close the gap is to strengthen her study behaviors for the second half of the term to increase the likelihood of getting As. She can make sure she attends every class, stays totally attentive and engaged in every class, takes great notes, completes all of her reading and homework, and asks the teacher for additional support where she needs it (in other words, lots of intentional behavior change).

But Josie has another option for how she chooses to respond to the grade feedback. When feedback shows a gap, we also have a choice to stick with our current behavior and *adjust the goal* or desired state. Josie could say, *"Actually, I feel like I'm working really hard at school and doing everything I can. Maybe it's not realistic to strive for all As this year"* and adjust her goal to a mix of As and Bs. This concept is known as *goal revision*.

Goals and feedback are inextricably linked. As you know from earlier chapters, anytime you receive feedback, it is in relation to some goal, standard, or expectation. Once you receive the feedback it can be helpful to pause and reflect on what your goal is for acting on the feedback. In Josie's example, *she* owns that goal of what grades she is striving for. Presumably, she set the goal of getting all. As and she can own the decision to revise that goal. Similarly, when you receive feedback on some aspect of your behavior or performance and decide to act on it, you are working toward some goal or outcome. The question is: are you fully aware of and clear on that goal? Did you set the goal, or has someone else established it for you? You will likely have greater success and satisfaction working toward that outcome if you can articulate clearly what the goal is (and even better if you are fully bought into it, as opposed to simply doing what someone else wants).

Unclear goals muddy the waters of what exactly we are trying to achieve and why. One of the very worst goals that we can adopt is to simply "do our best." "Do your best" goals do not drive high performance or spark motivation because they lack specificity about what "good" looks like and they lack the necessary level of challenge that stretches people to higher performance. "Do your best" goals are ineffective because they create vague standards. If your boss tells you to "do your best," their expectation of "your best" may not be the same as your own, leading to a disconnect in expectations. Specificity is essential not only for feedback but also for effective goal, standard, and expectation setting. Research related to goal setting theory has consistently shown that specific goals that are difficult to accomplish drive higher performance (Locke, 1968; Locke & Latham, 2002). Goals that are challenging and specific require us to pull our behavior to higher levels; they drive us to exert more effort than easier goals, which have a lower motivational effect, or "do your best" goals, which provide little clarity or direction. However, this higher motivational effect depends on our level of ability and our commitment to the goal. If you set a goal that you simply do not have the ability to achieve, that goal is unrealistic. Similarly, if you set a goal that you aren't committed to achieving, you may not have the motivation and drive needed to achieve it. Sometimes, when feedback highlights a gap between our current performance and a challenging goal that we don't have the ability or commitment to achieve, adjusting the goal state can be a healthier and more productive alternative to ramping up our efforts.

Last year, two of my nieces set their annual goals for selling Girl Scout cookies. One of my nieces set an ambitious sales goal of 300 boxes of cookies. Her younger sister went a different direction, with a goal of selling eight boxes of cookies. Once the disparity of their goals became apparent, the girls came together and set a goal of each selling 120 boxes of cookies. Some social comparison and reflection on their initial commitments and attainability of their goals suggested one was a little too challenging, while the other was way too easy. In setting their revised shared goals, the girls also took stock of their sales opportunities—counting up family members and neighbors they could sell to. Comparing each goal against another outside standard (their sister's goal) provided feedback on their initial goals, which drove them to do some additional fact-gathering and calibration and ultimately revise their goals to something more realistic.

Goal commitment impacts how we respond when feedback highlights a gap between the current and desired level of performance (Carver & Scheier, 1998; Johnson et al., 2006; Vancouver, 2005). If my older niece had been deeply committed to her initial goal of selling 300 boxes of Girl Scout cookies, rather than adjusting her sales goal, she would have adjusted her behavior. She could have set up shop outside of a retail store or location where she would get foot traffic, above and beyond the family members and neighbors she counted on as likely customers. She could have persuaded her uncle to buy 25 boxes, rather than 10. But because her commitment to sell 300 boxes was not that strong, a revised goal of 120 was more realistic.

When Goals Collide

Sometimes making adjustments to close the gap between current and desired behavior is hard, not because of lack of motivation, lack of ability, or excessively difficult goals, but because we have *competing goals*. In their meta-analysis of the impact of technology on behavior change, Hermsen and colleagues (2016) found that feedback generated by technology can be highly effective for closing gaps related to lifestyle habits, such as eating less, eating better, exercising more, and reducing water and electricity consumption. They also found that feedback will not lead to behavior change when another competing goal is present. For example, if your water bills suggest you are consuming a large quantity of water in your home each month, and you care about conservation, you may cut back on long showers or watering your lawn. However, if you also have a goal of having a beautifully landscaped garden and lawn, that conservation goal could be compromised. If you are more committed to your goal of having a beautiful lawn than you are to your water conservation goal, you will likely not change your behavior. The feedback on your water bills may have increased your awareness of how much water you are consuming by watering your lawn all summer, but it will not drive behavior change if you have another competing goal that is more important to you (like having a beautiful lawn).

The concept of competing goals can be helpful for understanding what is getting in the way or preventing us from making progress on goals. Personally, I often experience tension between my goal of having a decent work/life balance and another goal of being highly responsive to clients and collaborators. When these two goals are at odds (e.g., when I am trying to take an afternoon off and have over 50 new emails from clients or colleagues), I feel tension in my body and negative emotions, like a sense of conflict or frustration. When competing goals surface, you once again have a choice about what to do. You can abandon one of the competing goals, revise one or both of the goals to be more aligned, or choose to do nothing and simply accept the gap between your current behavior and the lower-priority goal, chalking it up to the importance of your higher-priority goal. Using our water conservation example, you could reduce the conflict between your two goals by filling your garden with resilient plants that don't require frequent watering or installing rain barrels to use wastewater for watering your lawn. These changes enable you to harmonize your competing goals by reducing your water consumption without giving up on your goal of having beautiful landscaping. An alternative would be to revise your conservation goal to include more than only saving water, such as focusing instead on cutting carbon emissions by biking to work rather than driving and feeling less guilty about your water consumption as a result.

Goal abandonment is another viable option when feedback highlights a gap between our current and desired state (see Figure 5.2). In their discussion of strategies for dealing with goal discrepancies, researchers Campion and Lord (1982) note that goal abandonment is a very adaptive choice, but people are generally afraid to let go of goals, for fear of looking bad or feeling like they've given up. Hanging on to a goal that is no longer serving you, has no chance of being achieved, or is no longer relevant is completely unproductive. In instances like these, a moment of

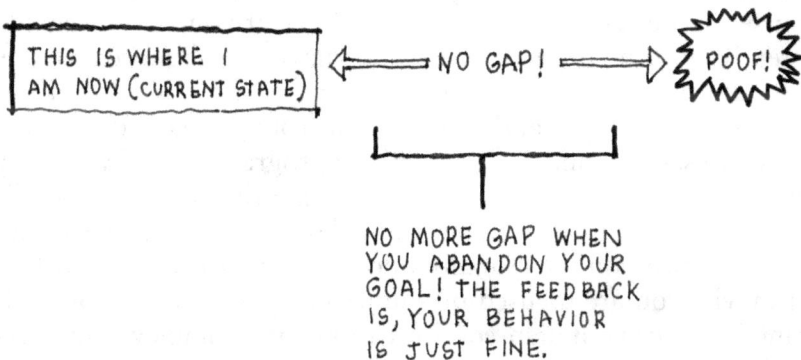

Figure 5.2 No longer a discrepancy when you abandon the goal!

feedback can be a useful catalyst to pause and evaluate whether or not a goal is still worth pursuing, or if you should give it up and focus your time and energy on a goal that is more important or that you're more committed to. Goodloe, the professional artist we met in Chapter 2, finds that abandoning or revising a goal gives him the freedom to truly create:

> Sometimes I will have a vision for what I want. I will paint this character and find that it doesn't match the expectation I had. I find expectations can be an enemy. Sometimes you have to start with what's there and let it develop, to exit the critical mode and pay attention to what's right in front of you. Letting go of expectations and the critical voice allows me to get into flow.

Your work and life are full of goals waiting to be abandoned. If you set a goal of having meeting-free Fridays and every Friday is back to back with meetings, the discrepancy between your goal and what is actually happening is probably creating some disappointment, frustration, or even feelings of failure for you. If those Friday meetings are important and you simply cannot move them to another day, abandoning your goal of meeting-free Friday might feel liberating. Or, instead of abandoning the goal entirely, you might consider revising the goal to be more realistic, such as not having meetings after 12 pm on Fridays, or having one meeting-free Friday per month. Perhaps you have a goal of learning to speak Spanish. You downloaded a language app to your phone and had good intentions of practicing every day. And every day, you see those reminders and ignore them. If you have been consistently ignoring those reminders and have gone hundreds of days without actually practicing Spanish, maybe now is a good time to abandon that goal and free yourself from the daily disappointment and self-judgment of not making progress toward your goal. Or perhaps you postpone the goal to another time in your life when it is more realistic and attainable, like after a big project ends, or once you have finally booked that trip to Mexico City. Or maybe you are focused on the wrong goal, if what you really want is to speak Italian so you can go on a Stanley Tucci-style food tour of Italy.

Goal abandonment and goal revision can be both practical and liberating when used wisely. Once we decide that a goal is attainable, goal *pursuit* is what enables us to close the gap between where we are and where we want to be. The key here is to get clear on what gap you want to close, why it's important, and what that means in terms of adopting new habits or changing your behavior. Sometimes, breaking goals down into smaller subgoals can help us take those first steps toward behavior change, particularly when the goal feels daunting.

Break Goals Down to Feel More Manageable

Although big, difficult goals are powerful for motivating and driving performance (Locke, 1968; Locke & Latham, 2002), smaller goals along the way break down intimidating goals into manageable steps and also provide the satisfaction of achievement in shorter increments. We know from goal setting theory that failing to make sufficient progress toward goals can be a major demotivator (Carver & Scheier, 1998; Johnson et al., 2006; Vancouver, 2005). Setting microgoals along the way enables us to track progress and feel the motivational pull of satisfaction from achieving small milestones. For example, most marathon training programs rely on microgoals to break down the big, daunting goal of running 26.2 miles into manageable milestones. These microgoals keep training healthy and realistic by focusing on incremental benchmarks that gradually increase over the course of several months. A less experienced runner may begin with runs of 2–3 miles several days per week and eventually build up to weekly long runs of 10–12 miles, and in subsequent weeks, all the way to 22–24 miles. This slow build enables runners to feel a sense of achievement with each milestone, to develop their running condition and ability at a safe and healthy pace, and ultimately achieve their goal of running a full marathon. Goal achievement is not slowed or stunted by the use of incremental goals; rather, progress toward big goals can feel more manageable and satisfying with milestones along the way. As each microgoal is achieved, we get a burst of motivation and self-efficacy to carry on. As a runner in training proves to herself she can run 10 miles, she starts to believe that she can run a half marathon. As she surpasses 18 miles, suddenly 26.2 seem attainable. Microgoals provide mini control loops that provide positive feedback each time a microgoal is achieved, fueling motivation and progress along the way to achieving the higher-order goal.

If you're really having trouble making progress on a goal, *implementation intentions* take microgoals to the next level. Implementation intentions help users articulate exactly what they will do, when, and how. Typically, intentions alone translate to behavior change only 20–30% of the time (Gollwitzer, 1999), which is why things like New Year's resolutions often fizzle out within a few weeks. But implementation intentions are not just "good intentions," they are concrete, actionable plans that enable the user to take simple steps to get closer to their goals. They function as "if/then" statements, prompting the user to plan "when situation X arises, I will do Y" (Gollwitzer, 1999). Implementation intentions can be especially helpful when we are procrastinating or struggling to get started on a new behavior. For example, let's say feedback in your annual review suggested that you need to work on your listening skills. Your ultimate goal is to be a better listener. That's a big goal that requires some challenging behavior change. A microgoal could be to talk less and listen more in each of your 1:1 meetings and calls at work. That's still a great intention, but it can be very challenging to break habits like interrupting, taking up more airtime than others, or thinking about how you will respond instead of really listening.

Implementation intentions can help. In this situation, you might set the implementation intention of *when I'm in 1:1 calls with my direct reports and I feel the urge to interrupt, I will pause and count to 5 before saying anything.* Or *I will open all of my 1:1 calls asking my direct reports first what is on their mind and what they want to discuss on our call.* Implementation intentions work because they prompt us to think through a future situation before it arises, and we therefore go into the experience more prepared and with a vision for how we will behave. Figure 5.3 shows an example, and Appendix E includes a worksheet to help you break one of your goals into microgoals and implementation intentions. Implementation intentions help bridge the gap between goal

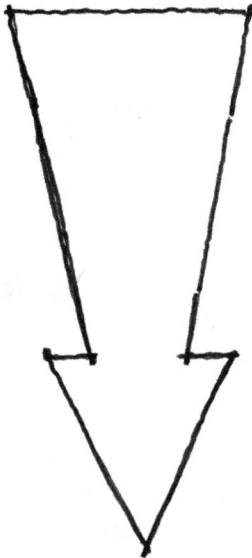

GOAL

RUN A MARATHON

MICROGOALS

WEEKLY MILESTONES -
3 MILES, 6 MILES, 10, 12,
18, ETC.

IMPLEMENTATION
INTENTIONS

WHEN I GET UP ON MONDAY,
WEDNESDAY, AND FRIDAY,
I WILL PUT ON MY RUNNING
CLOTHES AND COMPLETE MY
RUNNING PLAN BEFORE I GO
TO WORK.

Figure 5.3 Achieve tough goals by setting microgoals and using implementation intentions.

setting and taking action toward those goals through small steps forward.

Experiment With Behavior Change

Once we have identified the gap we want to close and the goal that we are willing to commit to, the next step is to select behaviors to experiment with in support of that goal. The ultimate goal of feedback is to drive some change in behavior—more of something, less of something, or something different entirely—and that is where the magic happens and also where we encounter some of the biggest challenges. Translating feedback into new behaviors is not always straightforward and can be difficult to put into practice. Behavior change requires self-awareness and an ability to see the nuances of our current behavior and how we need to adjust it. Behavior change also demands that we become aware of our habits and patterns and do the hard work to modify them.

As you'll recall from previous chapters, specificity is especially helpful for translating feedback into new behaviors. The more specific feedback is, the easier it is to identify the precise behaviors that we need to adjust (Ilgen et al., 1979). Feedback is always given in relation to some standard (or expectation or goal) that the feedback provider has in mind. Those standards are not always clear-cut and simple. At times, we may have multiple standards, which can feel in competition and muddy the waters as we work toward behavior change. A self-set standard that you hold may not be consistent with a standard that someone else has for you. For example, you and your kids may have different standards about what it means for a room to be "clean." You and your boss may have two different interpretations of a particular performance expectation. Standards also come in different levels of abstraction, ranging from broad and overarching to very specific.

For example, being "a good person" may be at the top of your personal standards hierarchy (high level of abstraction, broad). All of the specific, micro behaviors that ultimately add up to being a good person reside at the lower end of that hierarchy (lower level of abstraction). These are the things that we do on a day-to-day basis that all add up to being a "good person." When feedback and standards are too high level or abstract, they are harder to translate into specific actions and behaviors. Let's refer back to an earlier example about someone getting feedback on their "executive presence." Telling a leader they don't have executive presence is very abstract. Feedback delivered at such a high level of abstraction puts the burden on the recipient to figure out what exactly what they need to do or not do, which can feel like a lot of work, and also comes with a lot of uncertainty and ambiguity. Feedback at a lower level of abstraction that focuses on specific, observable behaviors makes taking action and changing behaviors much easier. In the executive presence example, that might sound like, "you looked at the floor during your entire presentation" or "you read directly from a script." You can see where those two specific behaviors are much easier to do something about than the abstract statement of "you lack executive presence." Box 5.2 features a concept called *distinctions* that can help us be clearer and more specific.

Box 5.2 Distinctions

Distinctions enable us to tell one thing apart from other, related things (Flaherty, 2010). Making distinctions between two very different things is easy. If you have a basic understanding of fruit, you can make distinctions between apples and oranges. You can eat the skin of apples; they are usually red or green and have a crisp texture. Oranges must be peeled to be eaten; they are typically orange in color and have juicy, pulpy texture. The more expertise we have on a topic, the more precise our distinctions become. For example, an apple grower will be able to make more specific distinctions between types of apples than most people, such as differentiating between Gala, Honeycrisp, and Fuji apples on sight and taste alone. In the context of feedback, distinctions can help us identify specific things we are doing or not doing in our behavior. A leader with deep expertise on a topic can make distinctions in an employee's work that the employee may not notice. Distinctions also enable behavior change by helping us figure out exactly what we need to do differently and why. If a golf coach provides feedback that makes a distinction between the student golfer swinging their arms versus swinging from their core, this could lead to a breakthrough for a developing golfer struggling with their swing. By suddenly understanding the difference between swinging with their arms versus their torso, this developing golfer now sees clearly what they have been doing wrong and what they need to do differently on every future swing. When it comes to behavior change, distinctions can help us identify exactly what we want to do differently and why.

The process of behavior change is iterative: You identify something you want to try, then you try it, notice what happened, reflect, maybe get some additional feedback, and decide what to try next, which might be the same thing again or something slightly different. Let's say you want to master the art of making a dry martini. You had a party last week and tried making drinks, but your friends didn't really seem to enjoy them, based on the feedback of many untouched drinks left on the kitchen counter throughout the evening[2] (but they did drink all the wine, so it must have been something about your cocktails). For your first step, you find a recipe that seems like a good starting point: gin, dry vermouth, and green olives. You make a batch of martinis, give it a taste, notice how the ingredients blend together, reflect on what you might want more or less of, and then adjust your recipe. Next time, you decide gin isn't really the flavor profile you're going for, so you switch to vodka. You make another batch, taste, notice, and reflect. Maybe a lemon peel would be closer to what you want than green olives. So next time you make martinis you try vodka, dry vermouth, and a lemon peel. You are pleased, so you decide to get some feedback. You invite a few of the same friends over again and ask them this time to give you feedback on your new martini recipe. You pour the drinks. They taste; you can see the wheels turning in their mind. Feedback! One friend says, "It's a 10/10—perfect." Another says, "I think it's very smooth and cold and balanced, but the problem is I just don't really like martinis." The third friend agrees that the balance of the ingredients is just right, and they ask you for your recipe (always great feedback when someone wants to replicate your behavior or approach). This likely feels like a frivolous example compared to the challenge of making changes that impact our work and relationships, but this simple example demonstrates how iterative change works. So now let's look at a more complex example.

Imagine for your whole life, you have had a pattern of getting emotionally triggered and reacting in ways that you later regret, such as yelling at your partner or team members in times of high stress. If you are lucky, your partner or colleagues will be brave enough to share specific and behavior-based feedback with you about your actions and the impact that it has on them. Assuming you take their feedback and decide you want to do something about it, the next thing you need to do is set a goal for how you'd like to change your behavior, such as "I want to stop yelling at people when I get upset" or, "When I get triggered, I want to take a deep breath and count to ten before saying or doing anything else."

The next step is to work on changing that behavior, which requires finding opportunities to practice, noticing or catching yourself in the act, and then trying something else. In our book, *The Coaching Shift* (2022), my co-author, Shonna Waters, and I outline a three-step process for breaking our historical "stimulus/response" patterns. In this example about wanting to stop yelling at people, the stimulus would be certain situations that make you feel triggered or hijacked, and the response is yelling. Our three-step process instead asks you to (1) notice, (2) pause, and (3) choose a different behavior. Undoing years of habit and stimulus/response behavior is hard, and takes deliberate, intentional practice. Inserting that pause (step 2) is critical for giving you a moment of self-aware reflection to choose a different behavior (taking a deep breath and counting to ten), rather than immediately defaulting to your historical behavior (yelling).

As you put feedback to work by making changes in your behavior, develop a habit of pausing to reflect on what is working and where you are having challenges. What breakthroughs did you experience that made you feel excited and validated in your behavior change? What old habits, expectations, or situations are holding you back from making lasting changes in your behavior? What other goals are competing with your behavior change goals? Reflection is a critical component of behavior change that enables us to update our mental models and incorporate new learning and experiences into our knowledge structures (Gray, 2007). Like visualization, reflection can reinforce and cement new attitudes, and attitudes that are developed with effortful thinking are more likely to translate to future actions and behaviors (Anseel et al., 2009; Petty et al., 1997).

In the context of behavior change, the reflection process can be even more powerful when it is coupled with . . . you guessed it . . . more feedback. Specifically, research by Frederik Anseel and colleagues showed that feedback was more effective for driving behavior change when it is coupled with reflection, and reflection is most powerful for driving behavior change when it is coupled with more feedback. High impact behavior change comes about through an ongoing process of trying out new behaviors, pausing to reflect on the impact of those behaviors, and getting additional feedback to assess the impact of the behavior for closing in on goals.

Get Support From Others

Feedback is not a solo experience. People generously provide it, often despite their own discomfort. And the way we respond to and use feedback impacts others. We also have the ability to enroll others to support us as we act on and apply feedback in our lives. For instance, 360-feedback assessments are most effective when the recipient works through the feedback with someone else, such as a professional coach. Researchers have found that working through 360 feedback with a facilitator or coach leads to setting higher development goals, creating specific action plans, and attaining higher subsequent performance (Seifert et al., 2003; Smither et al., 2003). Having an objective partner, such as a facilitator or coach, enables 360-feedback recipients to be open and honest as they explore their feedback, to reflect on how their self-assessments differ from others' perspectives, and to plan—in a non-judgmental environment—how they will follow through and take action on their feedback. Research has shown that 360 feedback is more likely to result in behavior change when users have support working through the feedback and establishing goals and plans for follow up (Anseel & Sherf, 2024). 360-feedback reports are often extensive and can feel overwhelming, so working with a professional coach to talk through, digest, make sense of, and prioritize the feedback helps make the experience feel more manageable and less isolating.

Adam, the Global Leader of Learning and Talent at a large multinational organization, shared an example of supporting leaders to make the most of a 360-feedback experience:

> We ran a development program where 100 of our top leaders participated in a 360 assessment. Our organization doesn't have a strong feedback culture, so I knew it was important to make sure the leaders felt safe and supported for this experience to work. The leaders attended a two-hour workshop before they received their 360 feedback reports. We sought to build trust and psychological safety with them. We set the tone that all leaders have both strengths and things to work on. We talked through the intention of the feedback and what to expect from the process. We provided time for them to share their concerns and ask questions. We helped them navigate the feedback and figure out what to do with it. Many leaders came up to me afterward and told me it was the most impactful development experience of their career because they had never received feedback like that before, that really helped them understand their behavior and how they are impacting others.

Coaching and feedback go hand in hand, and not just for formal feedback processes like 360s. Coaches—whether professional executive coaches or simply managers or colleagues who bring a "coaching approach" to their exchanges (e.g., deep listening, asking open-ended questions, reflecting back what they are hearing)—can help others work through the feedback they have received by talking through initial emotions and reactions and delving into creative problem solving. Coaching, with its focus on behavior change, growth, and outcomes, is perfectly suited to helping people do something with feedback and tie it to their personal growth goals. People who have a strong feedback orientation tend to be more open to coaching, *and* coaching can help to develop and strengthen feedback orientation over time (Gregory & Levy, 2012; Linderbaum & Levy, 2010).

Receiving feedback can feel lonely and isolating, particularly if it is overwhelming, challenges your self-perceptions, or is daunting to implement. But like asking directly for feedback, asking for support can eliminate some of the mystery and isolation. Asking for coaching support is one option, and that support can also come from colleagues, friends, family, or the person who provided the feedback in the first place. Following up and demonstrating accountability show that you have taken the feedback seriously. Letting the feedback provider know that you are doing something with the feedback can help to build your relationship and also strengthen *their* feedback orientation because they see that their feedback matters—that you are using it and doing something with it. Once they provide you with feedback, they are "in it" with you and, if you trust them and value their perspective, they can be a helpful source of support and thought partnership. As you work on new habits or behaviors, proactively seeking feedback from others lets them know that you are deliberately trying to change and gets them bought in to your development.

Figure 5.4 includes a recap of the five steps for putting feedback to use. The process of receiving feedback, digesting it, making sense of it, and deciding what to do with it can feel hard. Figuring out how to turn the feedback into new behaviors is also hard. And guess what: You can do hard things! My goal in this chapter is to normalize and acknowledge that receiving and using feedback is a challenging process and is also one of the best ways to learn, grow, stretch, and discover just how much you are capable

---

PUTTING FEEDBACK TO USE:

① DECIDE WHAT TO DO WITH THE FEEDBACK
② IDENTIFY THE GAP YOU WANT TO CLOSE
③ BREAK GOALS DOWN TO FEEL MORE MANAGEABLE
④ EXPERIMENT WITH BEHAVIOR CHANGE
⑤ GET SUPPORT FROM OTHERS

Figure 5.4 Recapping the five steps for putting feedback to use.

of. Graciously receiving feedback and pulling others into your behavior change efforts is also a great way to build trust, credibility, and relationships with your colleagues, friends, and family members. One thing I want you to remember is just how much choice you have at every step of the feedback process. You ultimately get to choose whether or not you accept the feedback that you receive. Then, you get to choose what you do with it and how you act on it. You choose who you want to involve in that process. In some situations, you might feel an obligation to certain people (e.g., your boss or your partner) that limits your range of options, but you can feel more empowered and have a sense of ownership by identifying what you have control over and where you have choice.

Wrapping Up: Embracing Your Inner Feedback Zealot

Deciding to value and appreciate feedback is also a choice. Even if you still struggle to give, receive, ask for, or use feedback, you can choose to embrace feedback and commit to developing your feedback orientation and helping others do the same. After reading this book, I hope you recognize that feedback is so much more than just formal "events," like performance reviews, and it shows up in every part of our lives, not only at work. Ultimately, feedback provides helpful, useful, eye-opening data on ourselves. What a gift! (I know the saying "feedback is a gift" is overused, but really, getting all this data about yourself *is* a gift, particularly when people put themselves into a place of discomfort and self-doubt to share those data with you.) Some of the most useful feedback is mundane and you may not even recognize it as feedback. Think back to my list of 25 feedback moments from Chapter 1. Hardly any of those examples were "big deal" feedback, like a performance review or an uncomfortable interaction. We are constantly surrounded by data and information from other people—from our inner monologue, from technology, and from our environment—that help us understand ourselves relative to the world around us. One goal of this book was to shift the way you think about feedback—where it comes from, what it looks like, how it is presented, and how often we receive it.

One way to become more comfortable with feedback is simply to engage with it more often. Try a 30-day feedback challenge and see how it impacts your comfort level with feedback. Every day for 30 days, challenge yourself to give, ask for, or use feedback at least once per day (there's a worksheet in Appendix F to help you). This exercise will make you more aware of the feedback around you and also give you opportunities to practice, which is a critical part of behavior change. You can practice in any context—at work, with your family, with your friends. *Tell* the barista at your local coffee shop that when they fill your coffee to the very top you don't have room to add milk and then it spills all over you. Poof—done with your feedback challenge for the day. (Also, this is a great example of where you can make your feedback actionable by following it with a direct request, such as "Can you please leave room for me to add milk?" or "Can you please pour some of this into the sink for me?") After your next 1:1 with a team member or colleague, *ask* them, "What was most useful in our conversation today?" or "What is one thing I can do to better support you?" Practice asking for feedback in a way that makes it easy for others to respond by using open-ended, specific questions, which also increase the likelihood that you'll get specific feedback in return. If you're looking for a piece of feedback to act on, start by noticing feedback you have received recently, whether it's from family, colleagues, technology, and even your own inner monologue. Pick something that feels actionable and meaningful to put to *use*. One of my favorite stories of acting on feedback came from author and interior and plant designer Hilton Carter (2025). One day his neighbor from the apartment next door knocked on his door to tell him his music was too loud. Not only did he accept and use that feedback by turning the music down, but he also asked her to go back to her apartment so they could do a sound check and determine at what volume level she could hear his music. He committed to never turn the music up above that volume level.

If you feel really inspired, bring the 30-day feedback challenge to your organization. Encourage your colleagues to join you in sharpening those feedback skills each day. In addition to practicing, share a weekly tip on feedback best practices to help others develop their feedback orientation and keep feedback top of mind.

We are immersed in a sea of feedback—we can find it all around us, all the time. Without it, we would wander aimlessly toward (or away from) our goals, unsure of where we stand, what we are doing right, and where we are off course. Feedback is not only a valuable source of information but also a critical form of communication that, when given effectively, can build and strengthen relationships and connections, and when given poorly, can undermine trust and chip away at relationships. Feedback can be challenging to give, accept, and use, but it becomes more manageable when we apply what we've learned from behavioral science.

The beauty of the concepts in this book is that you can use them immediately. You can even apply what you learned about goal setting and implementation intentions to help you. Try this:

> Next time [situation where I want to provide feedback] arises, I will pause to think about the feedback I want to provide. I will plan what I want to say, making it behavior-focused and specific. I will say it, and then stop talking, giving the other person time to process and respond.

Build your feedback-seeking muscles by identifying a goal you are working on that is important to you and make a point tomorrow to ask someone whose opinion you trust for feedback on your behavior related to that goal. Try,

> [Person's name], I am working to achieve [this goal] and want to get some outside perspective on how I'm doing. Based on what you've observed, what's one thing you think I'm doing that is helping me get closer to that goal, and one thing you think I could do differently or stop doing to help me get closer to that goal?

Every time you give effective feedback, ask someone else for feedback, and pause to think about, accept, and find the value in that feedback, you are strengthening your feedback orientation, and possibly the feedback orientation of whomever you're engaging with.

This book covered a lot of research and best practices. We established that all feedback exchanges consist of four parts: The source of the feedback, the recipient, the actual message, and the context in which it is provided (Gregory & Levy, 2015). We drew on decades of empirical feedback research that highlight the little nuances and tweaks that can set feedback up for maximum effectiveness. Here is my personal top ten list of favorite feedback tools and practices:

1. Always focus feedback on behavior (or the task), not the person.
2. Make your feedback as specific and evidence-based as possible.
3. Give feedback as soon as possible, but not in public.
4. Choose the most effective medium for your feedback, based on the situation and the person you're giving feedback to.
5. When you receive feedback, remember that you are 50% of the exchange—it's not happening *to* you. Don't be afraid to ask questions. Don't feel pressure to have a clever response in the moment. It's okay to take time to process.
6. When asking others for feedback, ask questions that are specific and open-ended to increase the likelihood that you get specific, high-quality feedback in return. Try using the "pre-ask."
7. Think about feedback in relation to your goals. Remember that all behavior is driven by goals, and feedback tells us how we're tracking against our goals. Negative process feedback can be some of the most helpful for figuring out how to close gaps.
8. When working on behavior change, remember that it's an incremental process. Focus on the next step you will take. Keep it manageable and celebrate every success.
9. Listen deeply and ask open-ended questions. This will serve you well in any feedback exchange, whether you are giving or receiving.

10. Remember that all feedback exchanges take place in the context of relationships past, present, and future. Your feedback interactions can either build and strengthen those relationships or erode them, depending on what you say and how you say it.

Self-reflection is a critical step for learning. It helps you pause to recognize and digest what you have learned. So, as we wrap up, here are a few reflection questions for you to consider:

How has your understanding of feedback evolved since you started this book?
What did you learn about feedback that was most surprising?
What were you already doing effectively in your own feedback practices?
What were you doing that wasn't so effective?
What will you change as a result of what you learned?
What are you excited to try out?

I love hearing from readers, so please feel free to reach me at feedbackfundamentals@gmail.com to share your stories, discoveries, feedback (how meta), questions, and more. Thank you for reading!

Try It

Try the 30-day feedback challenge. Really. Try it. There is a worksheet in Appendix F to help you. Then give yourself a reward for completing the challenge—maybe that's a visit to your favorite bakery, a fancy new water bottle, a massage, or something else that will feel special and meaningful to you.

Pro Tip

Although this is a book about feedback, goals play a leading role as well. As you work on implementing feedback best practices, look for opportunities to tune up your goal setting and striving practices. Take it from Matt Coursen, Executive Managing Director at the global commercial real estate firm JLL:

> For me, one of the most helpful concepts in this book was competing goals. Now I can recognize when I feel a sense of frustration or conflict, often it's a result of having two (or more) conflicting goals. When those situations arise, I take a few minutes to actually write down the different goals, figure out why they are at odds, and then identify a much more effective way forward than I would have otherwise. It helps me gain clarity, prioritize, and come up with better solutions.

Notes

1 People consistently overestimate how good they will feel and how their life will change when anticipating a positive event, like a major promotion or winning the lottery. When great things happen, people experience a short burst of positive emotion immediately after the experience but quickly revert back to "normal"—how they felt and behaved before the great event. This phenomenon is known as the "hedonic treadmill" (Brickman & Campbell, 1971). The same is also true about negative events: We consistently overestimate just how bad we will feel or how hard something will be but also quickly revert to "normal."
2 Noticing the untouched martinis is an example of monitoring—you surmised based on the untouched drinks that people didn't like them, as opposed to getting the direct feedback.

Appendix A: Apply Control Theory to Your Own Example

What is your goal, or a standard or expectation you're trying to meet?

What is your current state, or current level of performance?

What is the gap or distance between your current state and your goal or desired end state?

What feedback do you need to help you further assess that gap and how to close it?

Appendix B: Questions to Help You Apply the Four-Part Model to Feedback You Want to Give

Source (you)

What do you know about your level of trust and credibility with the other person?

How will you make it clear that your intention is to help and share useful data?

What needs to be true for you to be clear and direct in your feedback?

Message

What exactly do you want to say?

What do you want the other person to hear and understand from your feedback?

How can you make your feedback more specific and ensure it is focused on behaviors?

Context

When is the right time to share this feedback?

How will you share it (e.g., conversation, in writing, etc.)?

How will you bring it up with the other person?

Recipient

What do you know about how this person generally responds to feedback?

How will you invite them into the conversation, so it does not feel one-way?

What about this feedback will feel important to this person?

Appendix C: Apply the Situation-Behavior-Impact (SBI) Framework to Your Feedback

First, do some unconstrained free writing: What is the feedback you want to give, and to whom?

Don't overthink it or judge what you write—just get it out of your brain onto paper.

Now, make that feedback more structured and higher quality by applying the SBI framework.

What is the situation where you have observed the behavior?

What is the actual behavior you want to give feedback on?
Remember to be specific, evidence-based, and focused on observable behavior, not the person! Don't make inferences or assumptions about WHY they do it or what they are thinking.

What is the impact of their behavior?

If you want, you can also add the "D" for Desired Behavior, which could include an expectation or a request. What do you want to see them do (or not do) instead in the future?

Appendix D: A Framework for Setting Clear Expectations

Do [WHAT] to/for/with [WHOM] by [WHEN] to [WHAT STANDARD] and here's [WHY].

What do you want this person to do in the future? What is the behavior?

Who else is involved?

What's the timeline (by when?)?

What is the standard you are looking for? What does "good" look like?

Provide the "why"—what's important about this? What other context would be helpful?

Appendix E: Break a Goal Into Microgoals and Implementation Intentions

What is one goal that you have right now—work or personal?

Write that goal here:

Now, break that goal down into a few microgoals or subgoals. For example, if my goal was to write this book, I might break that down into smaller goals like complete the research, write Chapter 1, write Chapter 2, etc.

List your microgoals here (as many or as few as you want):

Continued on the next page

Pick one microgoal, particularly one that feels tough to get started on, and outline some implementation intentions for how you'll get started. For example, on my microgoal of completing the research for this book, I might have implementation intentions like:

> "On Thursday morning, block off 1 hour to find new articles published on feedback orientation seeking since 2019."
> "Every morning before my workout, read one new journal article and jot down some notes."

Write some implementation intentions here. Remember that specificity is the key to turning these into action:

Appendix F: Take the 30-Day Feedback Challenge!

Congratulations on deciding to take on the 30-day feedback challenge!

Your mission is to give, ask for, receive, or use feedback once per day, every day for 30 days.

Use this log to record your experiments and what you noticed.

Day	What did you try? (Give, ask for, receive, or use)	What did you learn or notice?
1		
2		
3		
4		
5		
6		
7		
8		
9		
10		
11		
12		

13		
14		
15		
16		
17		
18		
19		
20		
21		
22		
23		
24		
25		
26		
27		
28		
29		
30		

Now CELEBRATE! You did it! How will you reward yourself for completing the challenge?

References

Abi-Esber, N., Abel, J. E., Schroeder, J., & Gino, F. (2022). "Just letting you know . . ." Underestimating others' desire for constructive feedback. *Journal of Personality and Social Psychology, 123,* 1362–1385. https://doi.org/10.1037/pspi0000393

Adobe. (2017). *Performance review peril: Adobe study shows office workers waste time and tears.* https://news.adobe.com/press-release/corporate/performance-review-peril-adobe-study-shows-office-workers-waste-time-and

Ajjawi, R., & Regehr, G. (2019). When I say . . . feedback. *Medical Education, 53,* 652–654. https://doi.org/10.1111/medu.13746

Albright, M. D., & Levy, P. E. (1995). The effects of source credibility and performance rating discrepancy on reactions to multiple raters. *Journal of Applied Social Psychology, 25,* 577–600.

Alvero, A. M., Bucklin, B. R., & Austin, J. (2001). An objective review of the effectiveness and essential characteristics of performance feedback in organizational settings (1985–1998). *Journal of Organizational Behavior Management, 21,* 3–29.

Anseel, F., & Lievens, F. (2006). Certainty as a moderator of feedback reactions? A test of the strength of the self-verification motive. *Journal of Occupational and Organizational Psychology, 79,* 533–551.

Anseel, F., Lievens, F., & Schollaert, E. (2009). Reflection as a strategy to enhance task performance after feedback. *Organizational Behavior and Human Decision Processes, 110,* 23–35.

Anseel, F., & Sherf, E. (2024). A 25-year review of research on feedback in organizations: From simple rules to complex realities. *Annual Review of Organizational Psychology and Organizational Behavior, 12.* https://doi.org/10.1146/annurev-orgpsych-110622-031927

Anseel, F., Strauss, K., & Lievens, F. (2018). How future work selves guide feedback seeking and feedback responding at work. In D. L. Ferris, R. E. Johnson, & C. Sedikides (Eds.), *The self at work: Fundamental theory and research* (pp. 295–318). Routledge/Taylor & Francis Group. https://doi.org/10.4324/9781315626543-13

Ashford, S. J., Blatt, R., & VandeWalle, D. (2003). Reflections on the looking glass: A review of research on feedback-seeking behavior in organizations. *Journal of Management, 29*(6), 773–799.

Ashford, S. J., & Northcraft, G. B. (1992). Conveying more (or less) than we realize: The role of impression management in feedback seeking. *Organizational Behavior and Human Decision Processes, 53,* 310–334.

Atkins, P. W. B., & Wood, R. E. (2002). Self-versus others' ratings as predictors of assessment center ratings: Validation evidence for 360-degree feedback programs. *Personnel Psychology, 55,* 871–904.

Au, A. K. C., & Chan, D. K. S. (2013). Organizational media choice in performance feedback: A multifaceted approach. *Journal of Applied Social Psychology, 43,* 397–407.

Baker, N. M., Elicker, J., & Levy, P. E. (2025). *Does feedback modality matter? An investigation of the effects on reactions to negative feedback and the role of source credibility and employee implicit mindset.* [Master's thesis, University of Akron].

Bandura, A. (1986). *Social foundations of thought and action: A social cognitive theory.* Englewood Cliffs, NJ: Prentice Hall.

Barnes, C. D., Bullard, M. B., & Kohler-Evans, P. (2017). Essential coaching skills for affective development. *Journal of Education and Culture Studies, 1,* 176–185.

Barry, B., & Crant, J. M. (2000). Dyadic communication relationships in organizations: An attribution/expectancy approach. *Organizational Science, 11,* 648–664.

Bass, B., & Riggio, R. (2006). *Transformational leadership.* New York: Psychology Press.

Bernstein, E. S., & Li, S. (2017). Seeing where you stand: From performance feedback to performance transparency. *Academy of Management Proceedings, 1,* 14752.

Blair, A., & McGinty, S. (2013). Feedback-dialogues: Exploring the student perspective. *Assessment & Evaluation in Higher Education, 38*(4), 466–476. https://doi.org/10.1080/02602938.2011.649244

Bodenhausen, G. V., Kramer, G. P., & Suesser, K. (1994). Happiness and stereotypic thinking in social judgment. *Journal of Personality and Social Psychology, 66,* 621–632.

Bracken, D. W., Timmreck, C. W., Fleenor, J. W., & Summers, L. (2001). 360 feedback from another angle. *Human Resource Management, 40,* 3–20.

Brickman, P., & Campbell, D. T. (1971). Hedonic relativism and planning the good society. In M. H. Appley (Ed.), *Adaptation-level theory* (pp. 287–302). New York: Academic Press.

Brown, B. (2018). *Dare to lead.* Vermilion.

Brown, K. W., & Ryan, R. M. (2003). The benefits of being present: Mindfulness and its role in psychological well-being. *Journal of Personality and Social Psychology, 84,* 822–848.

Brown, S. P., Ganesan, S., & Challagalla, G. (2001). Self-efficacy as a moderator of information-seeking effectiveness. *Journal of Applied Psychology, 86,* 1043–1051.

Cabral, L., & Hortacsu, A. (2010). The dynamics of seller reputation: Theory and evidence from eBay. *Journal of Industrial Economics, 58,* 54–78.

Campion, M. A., & Lord, R. G. (1982). A control systems conceptualization of the goal-setting and changing process. *Organizational Behavior and Human Performance, 30,* 265–287.

Carter, H. (2025). *She came to turn the music down. She left with a husband.* Instagram post. https://www.instagram.com/p/DItQMKeMs7 G/?igsh=azQ5eWRqdjVkODB4

Carver, C. S., & Scheier, M. F. (1998). *On the self-regulation of behavior.* New York: Cambridge University Press.

Cawley, B. D., Keeping, L. M., & Levy, P. E. (1998). Participation in the performance appraisal process and employee reactions: A meta-analytic review of field investigations. *Journal of Applied Psychology, 83,* 615–633.

Chan, E., & Sengupta, J. (2013). Observing flattery: A social comparison perspective. *Journal of Consumer Research, 40,* 740–58. https://doi.org/10.1086/672357

Colquitt, J. A., LePine, J. A., & Noe, R. A. (2000). Toward an integrative theory of training motivation: A meta-analytic path analysis of 20 years of research. *Journal of Applied Psychology, 85,* 678.

Cooperrider, D. L., & Srivastva, S. (1987). Appreciative inquiry in organizational life. In R. W. Woodman & W. A. Pasmore (Eds.), *Research in organizational change and development* (Vol. 1, pp. 129–169). Stamford, CT: JAI Press.

Dahling, J. J., Chau, S. L., & O'Malley, A. L. (2012). Correlates and consequences of feedback orientation in organizations. *Journal of Management, 38*, 530–545.

Delavallade, C. (2021). Motivating teams: Private feedback and public recognition at work. *Journal of Public Economics, 197*, https://doi.org/10.1016/j.jpubeco.2021.104405

DeNisi, A. S., & Pritchard, R. D. (2006). Performance appraisal, performance management, and improving individual performance: A motivational framework. *Management and Organizational Review, 2*, 253–277.

Dochy, F. J. R. C., Segers, M., & Arikan, S. (2022). *Dialogic feedback for high impact learning: Key to PCP-coaching and assessment-as-learning.* New York, NY: Routledge, 2023. | Includes bibliographical references and index. https://doi.org/10.4324/9781003294139

Dominick, P. G., Reilly, R. R., & Byrne, J. (2004). *Individual differences and peer feedback: Personality's impact on behavior change.* Paper presented at the 19th annual conference of the Society for Industrial and Organizational Psychology, Chicago, IL.

Dweck, C. (2006). *Mindset: The new psychology of success.* New York: Random House.

Earley, P. C., Northcraft, G. B., Lee, C., & Lituchy, T. R. (1990). Impact of process and outcome feedback on the relation of goal setting to task performance. *Academy of Management Journal, 33*, 87–105.

Edmondson, A. C. (1999). Psychological safety and learning behavior in work teams. *Administrative Science Quarterly, 44*, 350–383.

Edmondson, A. C., & Bransby, D. P. (2023). Psychological safety comes of age: Observed themes in an established literature. *Annual Review of Organizational Psychology and Organizational Behavior, 10*, 55–78. https://doi.org/10.1146/annurev-orgpsych-120920-055217

Elfenbein, H. A. (2023). Emotion in organizations: Theory and research. *Annual Review of Psychology, 74*, 489–517.

Engelmann, J. B., Capra, C. M., Noussair, C., & Berns, G. S. (2009). Expert financial advice neurobiologically "offloads" financial decision-making under risk. *PLoS One, 4.* https://doi.org/10.1371/journal.pone.0004957

Flaherty, J. (2010). *Coaching: Evoking excellence in others.* New York, NY: Routledge.

Forbes Business Insights. (2025). *360-degree feedback software market size, share & industry analysis, by type, by application, and by regional forecast, 2025–2032.* https://www.fortunebusinessinsights.com/360-degree-feedback-software-market-104481

Fredrickson, B. L. (2001). The role of positive emotions in positive psychology: The broaden-and-build theory of positive emotions. *American Psychologist, 56*, 218–226.

Fredrickson, B. L. (2013). Updated thinking on positivity ratios. *American Psychologist, 68*, 814–822.

Gollwitzer, P. M. (1999). Implementation intentions: Strong effects of simple plans. *American Psychologist, 54*, 493–503.

Grant, A. (2021). *LinkedIn post.* https://www.linkedin.com/posts/adammgrant_withholding-feedback-is-choosing-comfort-activity-6802225987963695104-c_oT/

Gray, D. E. (2007). Facilitating management learning: Developing critical reflection through reflective tools. *Management Learning, 38*, 495–517.

Gregory, J. B., & Levy, P. E. (2008). *The effect of supervisor feedback orientation on subordinate perceptions of the feedback environment.* [Unpublished manuscript].

Gregory, J. B., & Levy, P. E. (2012). Employee feedback orientation: Implications for effective coaching relationships. *Coaching: An International Journal of Theory, Research and Practice, 5*, 86–99.

Gregory, J. B., & Levy, P. E. (2015). *Using feedback in organizational consulting.* Washington, DC: American Psychological Association.

Hall, D. T., Otazo, K. L., & Hollenbeck, G. P. (1999). Behind closed doors: What really happens in executive coaching. *Organizational Dynamics, 27*, 39–52.

Hammer, L. B., & Stone-Romero, E. F. (1996). Effects of mood state and favorability of feedback on reactions to performance feedback. *Perceptual and Motor Skills, 83*, 923–934.

Hays, M. J., Kornell, N., & Bjork, R. A. (2013). When and why a failed test potentiates the effectiveness of subsequent study. *Journal of Experimental Psychology: Learning, Memory, and Cognition, 39*, 290–296.

Hermsen, S., Frost, J., Renes, R. J., & Kerkhof, P. (2016). Using feedback through digital technology to disrupt and change habitual behavior: A critical review of current literature. *Computers in Human Behavior, 57*, 61–74.

Heslin, P. A., Latham, G. P., & VandeWalle, D. (2005). The effect of implicit person theory on performance appraisals. *Journal of Applied Psychology, 90*, 842–856.

Hosseini, S., Quan, J., Deng, X., Miyake, Y., & Nozawa, T. (2024). Avatar-based feedback in job interview training impacts action identities and anxiety. *IEEE Transactions on Affective Computing.* https://doi.org/10.1109/taffc.2024.3363835

Ilgen, D. R., Fisher, C. D., & Taylor, M. S. (1979). Consequences of individual feedback on behavior in organizations. *Journal of Applied Psychology, 64,* 349–371.

Johnson, R. E., Chang, C., & Lord, R. G. (2006). Moving from cognition to behavior: What the research says. *Psychological Bulletin, 132,* 381–415.

Katz, I. M., Moughan, C. M., & Rudolph, C. W. (2023). Feedback orientation: A meta-analysis. *Human Resource Management Review, 33.* https://doi.org/10.1016/j.hrmr.2023.100986.

Kauffman, C. (2006). Positive psychology: The science at the heart of coaching. In D. R. Stober & A. M. Grant (Eds.), *Evidence-based coaching handbook: Putting best practices to work for your clients* (pp. 219–254). Hoboken, NJ: Wiley.

Kluger, A. N., & DeNisi, A. (1996). The effects of feedback interventions on performance: A historical review, meta-analysis, and a preliminary feedback intervention theory. *Psychological Bulletin, 119,* 254–284.

Kraus, A. (2024). *Improving a feedback environment: An evaluation of a technology department's climate change intervention.* [Unpublished doctoral dissertation]. The University of Akron.

Levy, P. E., Albright, M. D., Cawley, B. D., & Williams, J. R. (1995). Situational and individual determinants of feedback seeking: A closer look at the process. *Organizational Behavior and Human Decision Processes, 62,* 23–37.

Levy, P. E., Cober, R. T., & Miller, T. (2002). The effect of transformational and transactional leadership perceptions on feedback-seeking intentions. *Journal of Applied Social Psychology, 32,* 1703–1720.

Li, A. N., & Tan, H. H. (2013). What happens when you trust your supervisor? Mediators of individual performance in trust relationships. *Journal of Organizational Behavior, 34,* 407–425.

Linderbaum, B. G., & Levy, P. E. (2010). The development and validation of the Feedback Orientation Scale (FOS). *Journal of Management, 36,* 1372–1405.

Locke, E. A. (1968). Toward a theory of task motivation and incentives. *Organizational Behavior & Human Performance, 3,* 157–189.

Locke, E. A., & Latham, G. P. (2002). Building a practically useful theory of goal setting and task motivation: A 35-year odyssey. *American Psychologist, 57,* 705–717.

Locke, E. A., & Latham, G. P. (2019). The development of goal setting theory: A half century retrospective. *Motivation Science*, 5(2), 93–105. https://doi.org/10.1037/mot0000127

London, M. (2003). *Job feedback: Giving, seeking, and using feedback for performance improvement.* Mahwah, NJ: Erlbaum.

London, M., & Smither, J. W. (2002). Feedback orientation, feedback culture, and the longitudinal performance management process. *Human Resource Management Review*, 12, 81–100.

London, M., Volmer, J., Zyberaj, J., & Kluger, A. N. (2023). Attachment style and quality listening: Keys to meaningful feedback and stronger leader-member connections. *Organizational Dynamics*, 52, https://doi.org/10.1016/j.orgdyn.2023.100977

Luca, M. (2016). *Reviews, reputation, and revenue: The case of Yelp. com.* Working Paper. Harvard Business School.

Matthews, G., & Wells, A. (1988). Relationships between anxiety, self-consciousness, and cognitive failure. *Cognition and Emotion*, 2, 123–132. https://doi.org/10.1080/02699938808408069

McCauley, C. D., Lombardo, M. M., & Usher, C. J. (1989). Diagnosing management development needs: An instrument based on how managers develop. *Journal of Management*, 15, 389–403.

McCrae, R. R., & Costa, P. T. Jr. (1987). Validation of the five-factor model of personality across instruments and observers. *Journal of Personality and Social Psychology*, 52, 81–90.

Medvedeff, M., Gregory, J. B., & Levy, P. E. (2008). How attributes of the feedback message affect subsequent feedback seeking: The interactive effects of feedback sign and type. *Psychologica Belgica*, 48, 109–125.

Mertens, S., & Schollaert, E. (2024). Leading by example: Supervisor downward feedback seeking, power distance, and the implications for the feedback environment. *International Journal of Business Communication*. https://doi.org/10.1177/23294884241277560

Meyer, J., Jansen, T., Schiller, R., Liebenow, L. W., Steinbach, M., Horbach, A., & Fleckenstein, J. (2024). Using LLMs to bring evidence-based feedback into the classroom: AI-generated feedback increases secondary students' text revision, motivation, and positive emotions. *Computers and Education: Artificial Intelligence*, 6. https://doi.org/10.1016/j.caeai.2023.100199.

Moss, S. E., & Sanchez, J. I. (2004). Are your employees avoiding you? Managerial strategies for closing the feedback gap. *Academy of Management Executive*, 18, 32–44.

Northcraft, G. B., & Ashford, S. J. (1990). The preservation of self in everyday life: The effects of performance expectations. *Journal of Personality and Social Psychology, 40*, 521–531.

Nurudeen, S. M., Kwakye, G., Berry, W. R., Chaikof, E. L., Lillemoe, K. D., Millham, F., Rubin, M., Schwaitzberg, S., Shamberger, R. C., Zinner, M. J., Sato, L., Lipsitz, S., Gawande, A. A., & Haynes, A. B. (2015). Can 360-degree reviews help surgeons? Evaluation of multisource feedback for surgeons in a multi-institutional quality improvement project. *Journal of the American College of Surgeons, 221*, 837–844. https://doi.org/10.1016/j.jamcollsurg.2015.06.017

O'Malley, A. L., & Gregory, J. B. (2011). Don't be such a downer: Using positive psychology to enhance the value of negative feedback. *The Psychologist Manager, 14*, 247–264.

O'Malley, A. L., Ritchie, S. A., Lord, R. G., Gregory, J. B., & Young, C. (2009). Incorporating embodied cognition into sensemaking theory: A theoretical integration of embodied processes in a leadership context. *Current Topics in Management, 14*, 151–182.

Pat El, R., Tillema, H., & van Koppen, S. W. M. (2012). Effects of formative feedback on intrinsic motivation: Examining ethnic differences. *Learning and Individual Difference, 22*, 449–454.

Pei, J., Wang, H., Peng, Q., & Liu, S. (2024). Saving face: Leveraging artificial intelligence-based negative feedback to enhance employee job performance. *Human Resource Management, 63*(5), 775–790. https://doi.org/10.1002/hrm.22226

Petty, R. E., Wegener, D. T., & Fabrigar, L. R. (1997). Attitudes and attitude change. *Annual Review of Psychology, 48*, 609–647.

Poulos, A., & Mahony, M. J. (2008). Effectiveness of feedback: The students' perspective. *Assessment & Evaluation in Higher Education, 33*, 143–154. https://doi.org/10.1080/02602930601127869

Pulakos, E. D., & O'Leary, R. S. (2011). Why is performance management broken? *Industrial and Organizational Psychology, 4*, 146–164.

Qian, J., Lin, X., Han, Z. R., Tian, B., Chen, G. Z., & Wang, H. (2015). The impact of future time orientation on employees' feedback-seeking behavior from supervisors and co-workers: The mediating role of psychological ownership. *Journal of Management & Organization, 21*, 336–349.

Ranard, B. L., Werner, R. M., Antanavicius, T., Schwartz, H. A., Smith, R. J., Meisel, Z. F., Asch, D. A., Ungar, L. H., & Merchant, R. M. (2016). What can Yelp teach us about measuring hospital quality? *Health Affairs, 35*, 697–705.

Rasheed, A., Khan, S. U. R., Rasheed, M. F., & Munir, Y. (2015). The impact of feedback orientation and the effect of satisfaction with feedback on in-role job performance. *Human Resource Development Quarterly, 26*, 31–51.

Reavis, R. D., Miller, S. E., Grimes, J. A., & Fomukong, A. N. N. M. (2018). Effort as person-focused praise: "Hard worker" has negative effects for adults after a failure. *The Journal of Genetic Psychology, 179*(3), 117–122. https://doi.org/10.1080/00221325.2 018.1441801

Results Coaching. (2025). *Powerful coaching: Level II.* https://www. resultscoaching.com/

Roberts, A., Levy, P. E., Dahling, J., Riordan, B., & O'Malley, A. (2019). *Feedback just ahead: The future of feedback is before us.* Symposium presented at the 34th Annual Meeting of the Society for I/O Psychology, National Harbor, MD.

Sedikides, C., & Strube, M. J. (1995). The multiply motivated self. *Personality and Social Psychology Bulletin, 21*(12), 1330–1335.

Seifert, C. F., Yukl, G., & McDonald, R. A. (2003). Effects of MSFB and a feedback facilitator on the influence behavior of managers toward subordinates. *Journal of Applied Psychology, 88*, 561–569.

Smither, J. W., London, M., Flautt, R., Vargas, Y., & Kucine, I. (2003). Can working with an executive coach improve multisource feedback ratings over time? A quasi-experimental field study. *Personnel Psychology, 56*, 23–45.

Smither, J. W., London, M., & Reilly, R. R. (2005). Does performance improve following multisource feedback? A theoretical model, meta-analysis, and review of empirical findings. *Personnel Psychology, 58*, 33–66.

Smither, J. W., & Walker, A. G. (2004). Are the characteristics of narrative comments related to improvement in multirater feedback ratings over time? *Journal of Applied Psychology, 89*, 575–581.

Sparr, J. L., & Sonnentag, S. (2008). Fairness perceptions of supervisor feedback, LMX, and employee well-being at work. *European Journal of Work and Organizational Psychology, 17*, 198–225.

Steelman, L. A., Levy, P. E., & Snell, A. F. (2004). The feedback environment scale (FES): Construct definition, measurement, and validation. *Educational and Psychological Measurement, 64*, 165–184.

Steelman, L. A., & Wolfeld, L. (2018). The manager as coach: The role of feedback orientation. *Journal of Business and Psychology, 33*(1), 41–53. https://doi.org/10.1007/s10869-016-9473-6

Tadelis, S. (2016). Reputation and feedback systems in online platform markets. *Annual Review of Economics, 8*, 321–340.

Taylor, M. S., Fisher, C., & Ilgen, D. (1984). Individual's reactions to performance feedback in organizations: Control theory perspective. In K. Rowland & G. Ferris (Eds.), *Research in personnel and human resource management* (pp. 81–124). Greenwich, CT: JAI Press.

Telio, S., Regehr, G., & Ajjawi, R. (2016). Feedback and the educational alliance: Examining credibility judgements and their consequences. *Medical Education, 50*, 933–942.

Thoebes, G. P. (2024). *Maximizing the effectiveness of negative feedback through mindfulness* [Doctoral dissertation, University of Akron]. OhioLINK Electronic Theses and Dissertations Center. http://rave.ohiolink.edu/etdc/view?acc_num=akron1731283479301191

Ungerleider, S. (2005). *Mental training for peak performance: Top athletes reveal the mind exercises they use to excel.* Emmaus, PA: Rodale Press.

Upshaw, J. D., Jr., Stevens, C. E., Ganis, G., Zabelina, D. L., & DiRusso, F. (2022). The hidden cost of a smartphone: The effects of smartphone notifications on cognitive control from a behavioral and electrophysiological perspective. *PLOS One, 17*(11), e0277220. https://doi.org/10.1371/journal.pone.0277220

van der Kleij, F. M., Eggen, T. J. H. M., Timmers, C. F., & Veldkamp, B. P. (2012). Effects of feedback in a computer-based assessment for learning. *Computers and Education, 58*, 263–272.

Vancouver, J. B. (2005). The depth of history and explanation as benefit and bane for psychological control theories. *Journal of Applied Psychology, 90*, 38–52.

Vancouver, J. B., & Morrison, E. W. (1995). Feedback inquiry: The effect of source attributes and individual differences. *Organizational Behavior and Human Decision Processes, 62*, 276–285.

VandeWalle, D., Cron, W. L., & Slocum, J. W., Jr. (2001). The role of goal orientation following performance feedback. *Journal of Applied Psychology, 86*(4), 629–640. https://doi.org/10.1037/0021-9010.86.4.629

Wang, B., Qian, J., Ou, R., Huang, C., Xu, B., & Xia, Y. (2016). Transformational leadership and employees' feedback seeking: The mediating role of trust in leader. *Social Behavior and Personality: An International Journal, 44*(7), 1201–1208.

Waters, S. D., & Riordan, B.G. (2022). *The coaching shift: How a coaching mindset and skills can change you, your interactions, and the world around you (1st ed.).* Routledge.

Waung, M., & Highhouse, S. (1997). Fear of conflict and empathic buffering: Two explanations for the inflation of performance feedback. *Organizational Behavior and Human Decision Processes, 71,* 37–54.

Weitzel, S. R. (2000). *Feedback that works: How to build and deliver your message.* Greensboro, NC: The Center for Creative Leadership.

Wells, A., & Matthews, G. (1994). Self-consciousness and cognitive failures as predictors of coping in stressful episodes. *Cognition and Emotion, 8,* 279–295. https://doi.org/10.1080/0269993940840894

Wessel, J. L., Lemay, E. P., & Barth, S. E. (2023). You(r behaviors) are racist: Responses to prejudice confrontations depend on confrontation focus. *Journal of Business Psychology, 38,* 109–134. https://doi.org/10.1007/s10869-022-09811-5

West, T. V., Thorson, K., Grant, H., & Rock, D. (2018). Asked for vs. unasked for feedback: An experimental study. *Neuroleadership Journal.* https://neuroleadership.com

Westerman, C. Y. K., Reno, K. M., & Heuett, K. B. (2015). Delivering feedback: Supervisors' source credibility and communication competence. *International Journal of Business Communication,* 1–21. https://doi.org/10.1177/2329488415613338

Westerman, C. Y. K., & Westerman, D. K. (2013). What's fair? Public and private delivery of project feedback. *Journal of Business Communication, 50,* 190–207. https://doi.org/10.1177/0021943612474991

Whitworth, L., Kimsey-House, K., Kimsey-House, H., & Sandhal, P. (2009). *Co-active coaching.* Boston, MA: Davies-Black.

Williams, J. R., & Johnson, M. A. (2000). Self-supervisor agreement: The influence of feedback seeking on the relationship between self and supervisor ratings of performance. *Journal of Applied Social Psychology, 30,* 275–292.

Winstone, N. E., Nash, R. A., Parker, M., & Rowntree, J. (2017). Supporting learners' agentic engagement with feedback: A systematic review and a taxonomy of recipience processes. *Educational Psychologist, 52,* 17–37.

Yang, B., Watkins, K. E., & Marsick, V. J. (2004). The construct of the learning organization: Dimensions, measurement, and validation. *Human Resource Development Quarterly, 15,* 31–55.

Yelp. (2025a). *Fast facts.* https://www.yelp-press.com/company/fast-facts/default.aspx

Yelp. (2025b). *Study shows high-intent consumers are contacting businesses quickly on Yelp.* https://business.yelp.com/resources/articles/

study-shows-high-intent-consumers-are-contacting-businesses-quickly-on-yelp/?domain=local-business

Zhang, J., Kuusisto, E., Nokelainen, P., & Tirri, K. (2020). Peer feedback reflects the mindset and academic motivation of learners. *Frontiers in Psychology, 11.* https://doi.org/10.3389/fpsyg.2020.01701. PMID: 32765378; PMCID: PMC7378527.

Index

For Product Safety Concerns and Information please contact our EU
representative GPSR@taylorandfrancis.com
Taylor & Francis Verlag GmbH, Kaufingerstraße 24, 80331 München, Germany